JumpStart™ Technology

Effective Use in the Solaris™ Operating Environment

John S. Howard
Alex Noordergraaf

Sun Microsystems Press
A Prentice Hall Title

Production Supervision: *Mary Sudul*
Acquisitions Editor: *Gregory G. Doench*
Editorial Assistant: *Brandt Kenna*
Cover Design Director: *Jerry Votta*
Cover Designer: *Kavish & Kavish Digital Publishing and Design*
Manufacturing Manager: *Alexis R. Heydt-Long*
Marketing Manager: *Debby vanDijk*

Sun Microsystems Press:
Marketing manager: *Michael Llwyd Alread*
Publisher: *Rachel Borden*

10 9 8 7 6 5 4 3 2 1

ISBN 0-13-062154-4

Sun Microsystems Press
A Prentice Hall Title

Acknowledgments

This book would not exist without the hard work and skill of Catherine M. Miller, who made it look so easy to exceed our every expectation and meet every request while always keeping a cheerful attitude.

A heart-felt thank you for the support and encouragement we received from "The Management": Bill Sprouse, Barbara Jugo, and Chuck Alexander. We would also like to thank Chuck Alexander for providing the vision as well as being the driving force to the Sun BluePrints™ program.

We are indebted to our technical reviewers, Doug Hughes and our colleagues throughout Sun: David Auslander, Don Bessee, David Bevans, Glenn Brunette, Tom Cox, David Deeths, Jim Falkner, Mark Garner, Aaron Kramer, Chris Kukkonen, Jason Reid, Nicki Sonpar, Keith Watson, and the engineers of the Install/Boot Technical Support Group of Sun's Americas Technical Assistance Center. Their comments, suggestions, and criticisms have helped make this a better book.

Thanks to Tim Marsh, the Enterprise Engineering Lab Manager, for obtaining the hardware we needed to research and validate this book.

We would also like to thank Terry Williams for creating the diagrams and graphics used in this book.

Finally, we like to thank our family and friends.

John S. Howard would like to thank his family—his mother Annette Howard, his sisters, Sue Howard and Cindy Christoffel, and his brother Bill Howard for the support that they have given him in this, and everything else he has have ever done.

Thank you to Tiffany Ribeiro and Chris Silveri, in addition to their support and friendship, their actions and good examples have taught him trust, respect and friendship.

Thanks to David Deeths and Mark Garner for providing guidance, suggestions, and friendship in addition to the excellent work they did reviewing the book.

John would also like to thank the following people, who have provided expertise, encouragement, support, friendship, understanding (when plans were cancelled to work on this book), and the good sense to laugh at his jokes: Andy Bowker, John ("jed") Dick, Richard Elling, Cydney Ewald, Kristi Herd, Ken Kambic, Brian Lovewell, and Gene Trantham.

Alex Noordergraff would like to say that without the support, encouragement, and love of his wife, Lisa, he would never have finished this book. Her understanding and tolerance were particularly invaluable when the writing was most difficult.

A heartfelt thanks to his father, Abraham Noordergraaf, for helping him see what he could do and to his mother, Gertrude Noordergraaf, for always being there and believing in him. Thanks also to his brother and sisters, Gerrit Jan, Annemiek, and Jeske for helping and supporting their youngest sibling.

Thanks also to Keith Watson for being both a friend and colleague.

Many thanks to Glenn Brunette without whom the Solaris Security Toolkit (formerly known as `jass`) would not be what it is today.

Thanks to his grandmother-in-law, Jewel Feierabend, for the cookies and cake on the weekends and to both her and Ralph for putting up with him when the writing wasn't going well.

Alex would also like to thank the following Sun colleagues for their understanding and help over the years: David Auslander, Debbie Behrman, Rob Diamond, Casper Dik, Ken English, Edmund Glover, Raymond Metzger, Alec Muffet, Cathleen Plaziak, Brad Powell, and John Ronga.

Contents

Preface

This book is one of an on-going series of books collectively known as the Sun BluePrints™ program. The *JumpStart™ Technology* BluePrint details best practices for facilitating and managing automated and consistent installations of the Solaris™ Operating Environment.

Sun BluePrints Program

The mission of the Sun BluePrints Program is to empower Sun's customers with the technical knowledge required to implement reliable, extensible, and secure information systems within the datacenter using Sun products. This program provides a framework to identify, develop, and distribute best practices information that applies across the Sun product lines. Experts in technical subjects in various areas contribute to the program and focus on the scope and usefulness of the information.

The Sun BluePrints Program includes books, guides, and online articles. Through these vehicles, Sun can provide guidance, installation and implementation experiences, real-life scenarios, and late-breaking technical information.

The monthly electronic magazine, Sun BluePrints OnLine, is located on the Web at http://www.sun.com/blueprints. To be notified about updates to the Sun BluePrints Program, please register yourself on this site.

Who Should Use This Book

This book is primarily intended for readers with varying degrees of experience or knowledge of JumpStart™ technology. Detailed examples of using JumpStart technology effectively every day are provided in combination with never-before-documented features and capabilities.

Before You Read This Book

You should be familiar with the basic administration and maintenance functions of the Solaris Operating Environment (hereafter, Solaris OE). You should also have an understanding of standard network protocols and topologies.

Since this book is designed to be useful to people with varying degrees of experience or knowledge of JumpStart technology, your experience and knowledge are the determining factors of the path you choose through this book.

How This Book Is Organized

This book is structured with Chapters 2 through 5 providing increasing depth into the configuration and use of JumpStart technology.

Depending on your level of experience and knowledge of JumpStart technology, you can skip Chapter 2 "JumpStart Overview," or use it as a review. If you are an experienced JumpStart user, you can skim Chapter 3 "JumpStart Customizations," or use it as a review.

Read the remaining chapters either sequentially for an overall comprehension of JumpStart or as your need dictates.

Chapter 1, "Introduction," provides a high-level overview of the structure and use of the JumpStart framework.

Chapter 2, "JumpStart Overview," presents the core components of the basic JumpStart architecture. The chapter focuses on how to get an automated JumpStart environment up and running as quickly as possible.

Chapter 3, "JumpStart Customizations" examines in depth the key components that were briefly touched on in Chapter 2, adding the information and recommendations necessary to best perform complex installations of the Solaris OE. Additionally, this chapter details the techniques and mechanisms necessary to provide the basics of how to extend the JumpStart framework to best suit the needs of your datacenter.

Chapter 4, "Postinstallation Procedures," builds on the advanced JumpStart technology techniques presented in Chapter 3 "JumpStart Customizations." It examines some of the lesser known (but more powerful) configuration options of the JumpStart application to perform a site-standard, hands-free installation of the Solaris OE and a hands-free installation of unbundled software applications, such as VERITAS Volume Manager (VxVM) and software patches. The chapter provides complete examples of automating the installation of the Solaris OE and additional unbundled (third-party) software applications.

Chapter 5, "Automating Installations," describes how JumpStart software installations can be automated through the use of repositories such as Dynamic Host Control Protocol (DHCP), Network Information System (NIS), Network Information System Plus (NIS+), files, and diskettes. To illustrate the configuration processes of these various JumpStart software techniques, this chapter presents a lab environment in which the various alternatives are implemented and described.

Chapter 6, "JumpStart Internals," applies the concepts presented in Chapter 2 and Chapter 3 to a SPARC-based automated JumpStart software installation by looking at the sequence of network traffic that was generated. The chapter examines the internals of the JumpStart technology process: its three phases based on the network protocols encountered.

Chapter 7, "JumpStart Security," recommends ways to securely incorporate the JumpStart framework into your environment.

Chapter 8, "WebStart Flash," provides an overview and tutorial on WebStart Flash, a powerful new facility of JumpStart technology available with the release of Solaris 8 4/01 (Update 4) OE. Flash can create a system archive (a snapshot of an installed system) and install the Solaris OE from that archive.

Chapter 9, "Customizing JumpStart Framework for Installation and Recovery," examines several of the more powerful, yet often overlooked, aspects of the JumpStart system. The chapter explains how to use JumpStart technology from a CD-ROM and how to extend the JumpStart framework into a platform for rapid system recovery.

Chapter 10, "Solaris Security Toolkit," details the Solaris Security Toolkit (Toolkit). This Toolkit automates the process of securing Solaris OE systems. In addition to its network-based or JumpStart-based mode, the Toolkit can also be run in standalone mode. This chapter focuses on the parts of the Toolkit used during a network or JumpStart-based software installation.

Note – The Solaris Security Toolkit was formerly known as the `jass` Security Toolkit.

Chapter 11, "System Cloning," refers to the rapid re-creation or reinstallation of a system. This chapter presents techniques for system cloning and rapid deployment of systems. This technique is especially useful in providing business continuity and disaster recovery.

Appendix A, "Using JumpStart Technology to Install Solaris OE for Intel Architecture," provides an example of using JumpStart technology to install Solaris 8 OE for the Intel Architecture on an Intel x86-based client from a Sun Enterprise™ E420r JumpStart server.

Glossary is a list of terms and acronyms used frequently in describing JumpStart technology.

Ordering Sun Documents

The SunDocs℠ program provides more than 250 manuals from Sun Microsystems, Inc. If you live in the United States, Canada, Europe, or Japan, you can purchase documentation sets or individual manuals through this program.

Accessing Sun Documentation Online

The `docs.sun.com` Web site enables you to access Sun technical documentation online. You can browse the `docs.sun.com` archive or search for a specific book title or subject. The URL is `http://docs.sun.com/`.

Typographic Conventions

The following table describes the typographic changes used in this book.

Typeface or Symbol	Meaning	Example
AaBbCc123	The names of commands, files, and directories; on-screen computer output	Edit your .login file. Use ls -a to list all files. machine_name% You have mail.
AaBbCc123	What you type, contrasted with on-screen computer output	machine_name% **su** Password:
AaBbCc123	Command-line placeholder: replace with a real name or value	To delete a file, type rm *filename*.
AaBbCc123	Book titles, new words or terms, or words to be emphasized	Read Chapter 6 in *User's Guide*. These are called *class* options. You *must* be root to do this.

Shell Prompts in Command Examples

The following table shows the default system prompt and superuser prompt for the C shell, Bourne shell, and Korn shell.

Shell	Prompt
C shell prompt	machine_name%
C shell superuser prompt	machine_name#
Bourne shell and Korn shell prompt	$
Bourne shell and Korn shell superuser prompt	#

## CHAPTER 1

Introduction

JumpStart technology was introduced by Sun Microsystems in 1995 to assist in the installation and automation of the Solaris Operating Environment (Solaris OE). JumpStart technology uses a client/server architecture. The server provides the JumpStart framework, and the client is the system on which the Solaris OE is installed.

This chapter provides a high-level overview of the structure and use of the JumpStart framework. The topics covered in this chapter are:

- Reasons for using JumpStart technology
- An overview of JumpStart technology
- A note on the examples in this book

For information on the structure of this book, please see the Section "How This Book Is Organized" in the Preface.

Reasons for JumpStart Technology

As datacenters grow in size, one of the most interesting and challenging problems facing datacenter personnel is how to retain consistency and control over systems while meeting the requirements of rapidly installing and deploying those systems. Over the past several years, software in general and operating systems in particular have increased in complexity. The installation and configuration of these complex software products is often labor intensive and correspondingly error prone.

JumpStart technology helps the system administrator manage complexity by fully automating the Solaris OE and system software installation, facilitating the correctness and standardization of systems and thereby enabling rapid deployment of hundred or thousands of systems. Further, since JumpStart technology minimizes the opportunity for human error during system installation, system availability may also be enhanced.

The advantages of using JumpStart technology are apparent in the area of system security. By using JumpStart technology with the Solaris Security Toolkit, discussed in Chapter 10, "Solaris Security Toolkit," a system can be secured during an automated Solaris OE installation. This helps ensure that system security is standardized and addressed from the moment of system installation, rather than being a last-minute task haphazardly done before a system is placed into production.

This book also examines the lesser-known, poorly understood, and previously undocumented aspects of JumpStart technology. As will be seen, these aspects of the JumpStart framework make JumpStart technology ideally suited for use as a platform for system recovery. It is a common misconception that JumpStart technology is only useful in installing a large number of systems. This book demonstrates that JumpStart technology can be just as useful in installing, deploying, and maintaining a small number of systems as it is in deploying hundreds or thousands of systems.

Overview of JumpStart Technology

JumpStart technology, occasionally referred to as the JumpStart framework, is a component of the Solaris OE, designed to facilitate installation of the Solaris OE. The most powerful aspects of JumpStart technology are its features to manage and automate the installation and to provide a mechanism to help ensure consistent installations of the Solaris OE.

Automation for Consistent Installations

JumpStart technology provides the mechanism to install the Solaris OE, either interactively or automatically (*hands-free*) from a *JumpStart server* to an *installation client*. This installation is performed with the Solaris OE product physically on the JumpStart server and transferred through the network to the installation client at the time of installation.

This network-based mechanism lends itself to installation of geographically dispersed systems. Additionally, because the installation can be fully automated, JumpStart technology is ideal for installing and deploying a large number of systems in a brief period of time. Further, because the information and choices used to install and configure the Solaris OE are on the JumpStart server, consistent Solaris OE installations can be maintained, regardless of geography or the time when the system was installed. There are many benefits to using JumpStart technology. Most obviously, they help to reduce errors in interactive installations, enable easy replication of systems, and help to minimize the time and costs associated with system installation.

The JumpStart Framework

The JumpStart framework provides two primary services. First, JumpStart application provides a framework to facilitate or completely automate all aspects of installation of the Solaris OE. Second, JumpStart technology provides a hardware-architecture-neutral Solaris OE kernel, called the miniroot. In addition to being used as the operating environment by the installation programs, the miniroot is also a fail-safe boot media. As a fail-safe boot media, the miniroot provides a stable and well-known operating environment from which to effect system recovery procedures.

JumpStart technology is based on a client/server architecture with a number of server components providing services throughout the installation process. From a high level, the components of a JumpStart system are the boot, configuration, and install server. TABLE 1-1 describes the components.

TABLE 1-1 JumpStart Server Components

Installation Client	Target system to be installed or upgraded
Boot server	Provides a fail-safe operating system (OS) to the installing client. The boot image is architecture neutral, affording base OS services to all hardware supported by that OS release.
Configuration server	Helps the client determine its unique profile. Partition sizes, the list of software to install, begin and finish scripts, etc., are all specified in a profile served by the configuration server.
Install server	Is the source of the software packages that are to be installed on the client.

In practice, all three JumpStart servers are often located on the same physical host, but that is not a requirement. Chapter 5, "Automating Installations," describes how these services can be distributed onto physically distinct servers and networks.

Booting a client over the network is initiated when that client broadcasts a Reverse Address Resolution Protocol (RARP) or Dynamic Host Control Protocol (DHCP) request.

Once the client is booted and the installation process has begun, the configuration and installation services use Network File System (NFS) to obtain the configuration files and the Solaris OE product to be installed.

The installation server can have multiple versions of the Solaris OE available to be installed. Additionally, the installation server can offer versions of the Solaris OE for architectures or platforms other than its own. For example, a Sun Fire 4800 can function as a JumpStart server for installation clients being installed with Solaris 8 4/01 OE for SPARC architecture, Solaris 6/00 OE for SPARC architecture, Solaris 2.6 OE for SPARC architecture, Solaris 8 6/00 OE for Intel Architecture, and Solaris 7 OE for Intel Architecture.

Examples

One of the our design goals for this book was to always provide complete *real-world* examples. This goal, along with the nonlinearity of this book, can result in some repetition of concepts. This repetition is considered to be an equitable trade-off for having complete and realistic examples in one place.

Note – Unless otherwise noted, all of the examples in this book are for the Solaris 8 4/01 (update 4) OE. Examples and concepts that have changed since previous releases of the Solaris OE are also noted.

All examples in this book have been validated by the authors in the Enterprise Engineering laboratory. Further, all scripts and example files examined in this book are available on the accompanying CD.

Summary

This chapter began by summarizing the rationale for JumpStart technology. It then provided a high-level look at that technology with a description of the client/server architecture of the JumpStart framework, the three services (boot server, configuration server, and install server) of a JumpStart server, and the mechanism and protocols employed by the JumpStart architecture.

A final section provided information about the examples in the book.

## CHAPTER 2

JumpStart Overview

This chapter presents an overview of the required core components of the basic JumpStart architecture. The chapter focuses on how to get a basic automated JumpStart environment up and running as quickly as possible.

This chapter describes the following topics:

- Boot process
- Server components
- Server directory architecture
- Server installation and configuration
- Installation automation
- Client installation and configuration

Note – Unless otherwise noted, the Solaris 8 Operating Environment 4/01 (update 4) is used.

Boot Process

To provide a better understanding of the JumpStart software process, this section reviews how a JumpStart installation for a SPARC system actually works.

RARP Request

Ok > boot net-install

1. When the `boot net - install` command is entered at the `ok` prompt, the JumpStart client looks for a JumpStart boot server.

2. The JumpStart client generates a Reverse Address Resolution Protocol (RARP) request.

3. A JumpStart server, on the local subnet, receives this RARP request and maps it to an Internet Protocol (IP) address, either through its `/etc/ethers` and `/etc/hosts` files or through a naming service, such as NIS, NIS+, or Lightweight Directory Access Protocol (LDAP).

4. In accordance with the IP address found, the JumpStart server generates a RARP reply to the JumpStart client.

5. The JumpStart server responding to the client's RARP request maps the client's media access control (MAC) address to its IP address and host name, returning this data to the client.

   This RARP packet also includes the IP address of the server providing the client with the JumpStart server IP address, which is used in the next phase of the process as the JumpStart boot server.

DHCP Request

With the release of the SPARC sun4u hardware architecture, it is possible to use Dynamic Host Configuration Protocol (DHCP), instead of RARP, to provide a JumpStart client with its IP address and other critical JumpStart information. DHCP can be used to dynamically provide a JumpStart client with an IP address and host name without requiring a local boot server. For the purpose of our example in this chapter, RARP is used. DHCP is detailed in Chapter 5, "Automating Installations."

Second-Level Boot Process

After the JumpStart client has an IP address, it can move to the second level of the network boot process.

1. The JumpStart client downloads a minimal Solaris OE kernel (called a miniroot) from the JumpStart boot server into the memory of the JumpStart client. This miniroot is downloaded by a Trivial File Transfer Protocol (TFTP) request issued by the JumpStart client.

   This TFTP request specifies the architecture of the miniroot and the IP address of the system requesting the miniroot on the server.

2. When the JumpStart boot server receives this TFTP request, it searches for a matching IP address and architecture in the `/tftpboot` directory.

3. After the JumpStart client is booted from the miniroot, JumpStart finds the `rules.ok` file.

   The entry is checked to make sure it matches that of the JumpStart client.

4. When a match is found, the actions specified are executed.

First, any specified begin scripts are executed. Then the specified Solaris OE profile is installed, and finally the finish scripts are executed.

Note – A `rules.ok` entry is required to specify, at a minimum, a profile.

When a new JumpStart client (`add_install_client`) is added to a JumpStart boot server, a file corresponding to its IP address and architecture is created in the `/tftpboot` directory. This file is actually a link to the generic miniroot for that Solaris OE version and architecture.

Now that the actual JumpStart client is booted, you can build a JumpStart server.

JumpStart Server Components

A successful JumpStart installation requires three types of services: boot, installation, and configuration. These three sets of services are provided on one or multiple servers but are usually located on the same physical server. Each type of service is described separately but installed on the same server in this example.

Boot Server

The JumpStart boot server provides the services most critical to a successful automated JumpStart software installation. The JumpStart server provides the following information:

- The client's IP address
- IP address(es) of both the JumpStart profile and install servers

A JumpStart boot server doesn't have to be separate from the configuration and install servers. However, it may have to be separate when RARP provides the IP address to a JumpStart client. The RARP protocol is not routed, so RARP requests are not forwarded by routers between subnets.

When DHCP is used, it is not necessary to have a JumpStart boot server on each network segment. However, DHCP requires a BOOTP relay server on each segment to forward DHCP requests to the DHCP server.

In wide area network (WAN) installations when RARP is used, it is necessary to have at least a boot server on each subnet. A more practical resolution to this problem, instead of having separate boot clients on each network segment, is to have either one boot or install server connected to multiple networks or to actually have a dedicated JumpStart network that a system is connected to *only* while doing JumpStart software installations on the same subnet. There are security concerns with connection to multiple networks; these are discussed in Chapter 7, "JumpStart Security."

Presented in Chapter 5, "Automating Installations," is an example of doing JumpStart software installations where the boot, configuration, and install servers are all on separate subnets. In addition, Chapter 5 offers an example of using DHCP to avoid the necessity of having a JumpStart boot server on the same network segment as the JumpStart client.

Configuration Server

One of the major benefits JumpStart technology affords is the ability to automate system installations so that the installation occurs without any human intervention. This is particularly important in large environments where new systems are always arriving and the ratio of systems to administrators is large, and in lights-out datacenter environments where there are no human operators and all operations are automated.

This configuration information can be provided through several different mechanisms. The minimum amount of information required to perform an automated JumpStart software installation is the following:

- host name
- IP address
- system locale
- time zone
- netmask
- IPv6
- terminal type
- security policy
- name service
- timeserver

If any of this information is not available from the configuration files on the configuration server or from a name service, the JumpStart software installation defaults to an interactive installation.

With the release of the Solaris 8 OE, not all of the required information can be specified through a name service. Specifically, the Internet Protocol version 6 (IPv6) and security policy configuration information (for example, whether security policies should be enabled or not) cannot be provided through NIS or NIS+ maps. The Solaris 8 OE does not support the use of LDAP as a repository for JumpStart configuration information. A `sysidcfg` file must be provided to the JumpStart client, with at least the IPv6 and security policy information, to fully automate the Solaris 8 OE JumpStart software installations.

A JumpStart configuration server provides the configuration information needed by a JumpStart client so that the JumpStart installation can continue without any interactive requests for additional information. In the `add_install_client` command, specify the configuration server to be used and a fully qualified path to the `sysidcfg` file. You run this command, detailed in "Client Definition" on page 31 of Chapter 3, on the JumpStart boot server.

Chapter 5, "Automating Installations," details the use of other repositories to automate JumpStart software installations.

Install Server

Another major piece of information provided to the JumpStart client by the JumpStart boot server is the `rules` file entry for the JumpStart client. The rules file can specify the script to be run before the Solaris OE installation, the profile used, and the script to be run after the OS installation. These parameters must be present in the `rules` file but can be placeholders (for example, a hyphen) and not specify actual scripts.

For maximal flexibility, the begin and finish scripts specified in the `rules` file are typically driver scripts used to call other scripts. Driver scripts provide a mechanism for a more modular JumpStart environment since they eliminate the need for one monolithic script.

The locations of the scripts and the profiles are specified in the `rules` file. In the recommended JumpStart architecture, (presented in the following section) all the JumpStart-related information is kept in a hierarchal directory structure to simplify management, version control, and backups.

Server Directory Architecture

The JumpStart process is divided into three different types of JumpStart servers. They are the boot server, the install server, and the configuration (or config) server. Each of the services offered by these servers can be on the same or separate systems. Regardless of the use of one or more systems, the recommended directory structure is the same on all the systems.

The recommended directory structure (see FIGURE 2-1) for the JumpStart server is a set of directory structures that logically organizes the required JumpStart server information in one place so that it can be easily maintained and managed by system administrators. For ease of maintenance, it is recommended that all of the JumpStart information be stored in dedicated filesystem partitions.

The root directory of these partitions is called /jumpstart throughout this book. It is in this base directory of the JumpStart server that the rules.ok file is stored. For this reason, the /jumpstart directory is used as the base directory for the install server option in the add_install_client command.

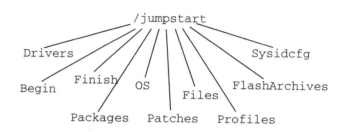

FIGURE 2-1 JumpStart Directory Hierarchy

Within the /jumpstart directory, create the following directories.

- Begin
- Drivers
- Files
- Finish
- FlashArchives
- OS
- Packages
- Patches
- Profiles
- Sysidcfg

The following sections briefly describe these directories.

Begin Directory

The Begin directory contains the scripts that are executed *before* the Solaris OE is installed on the JumpStart client. How, when, and why these scripts are written is detailed in "Scripting" on page 49 of Chapter 3.

`Drivers` Directory

The `Drivers` directory contains all driver scripts. Driver scripts are scripts listed in the `rules` files that call all other scripts during a JumpStart software execution. The driver scripts determine what modifications are made to each system by calling the appropriate finish scripts. The finish scripts perform the actual modifications to the Solaris OE on the JumpStart clients.

`Files` Directory

The `Files` directory contains files that are copied to the JumpStart client or referenced by the JumpStart client during installation.

`Finish` Directory

The `Finish` directory contains the scripts that perform system modifications and updates after the OS has been installed. Finish scripts can be written to perform various tasks, such as patch and software installation. How these scripts are written is detailed in "Scripting" on page 49 of Chapter 3 and in Chapter 4, "Postinstallation Procedures."

`FlashArchives` Directory

The `FlashArchives` directory is used in conjunction with the WebStart Flash extensions, released with Solaris 8 OE 4/01. This directory is a repository for flash archives, which are used as system images for Flash-based client installations. For additional details see "Creating and Administering Archives" on page 153 of Chapter 8.

`OS` Directory

The `OS` directory must contain *only* the Solaris OE files. These files are used by the JumpStart software, over the network, to build the client. Different Solaris OE releases should be stored in subdirectories within this subdirectory. The recommended naming convention for these subdirectories within `/jumpstart/OS` is `Solaris_<version #>_<4 digit-year>-<2 digit month>`. Since the installation process used in this chapter is based on Solaris 8 OE 4/01, the directory is named `Solaris_8_2001-04`. By creating different directories to store separate updates and releases of the Solaris OE, you can maintain fine-grained control for testing and deployment purposes.

A similar naming convention is used for Trusted Solaris OE. Specifically, `Trusted` is prefixed to the naming convention used above. Trusted Solaris OE version 8 12/00 would be stored in a directory called `Trusted_Solaris_2000-12`.

Optionally, when using architecture without SPARC technology, the architecture identifier should be appended to the end of the OS directory name. For example, the directory for Solaris 8 OE for Intel Architecture (IA) 4/01 is `Solaris_8_2001-04_IA`.

Packages Directory

The `Packages` directory should contain unbundled or third-party software packages to be installed by the finish scripts. For example, Secure Shell (SSH) software could be stored in the `Packages` directory so that the appropriate finish script can install and configure the software as required.

Patches Directory

The `Patches` directory contains all patches to be installed, including the Recommended and Security Patch Cluster, individual patches, and application patches. Subdirectories are created in the `Patches` directory for each of the Solaris OE versions being used. The patch clusters are extracted into the individual subdirectories.

Profiles Directory

The `Profiles` directory contains all the profiles. A profile is a file that contains configuration information used by the JumpStart software to configure the install client. The profile specifies such information as the Solaris OE package cluster to install (`Core`, `End User`, `Developer`, or `Entire Distribution`), the disk layout to use, and the type of installation to perform (for example, standalone). These configuration files define how specific systems or groups of systems are built.

`Sysidcfg` Directory

The `Sysidcfg` directory contains directories with OE- and host-specific `sysidcfg` files. Because of the OE-specific nature of the `sysidcfg` file, a generic version can no longer be used for all Solaris OE releases. The subdirectories use a naming convention similar to that recommended for the `/jumpstart/OS` directory (see "OS Directory" on page 11). The recommended installation convention is `Solaris_<version #>`. The `sysidcfg` files for the Solaris OE version 8 are stored in a subdirectory named `Solaris_8`. For different configurations with the same OE version, append a configuration identifier to the directory name. For example, a `sysidcfg` file to install the French version of Solaris 8 OE is stored in a directory named `Solaris_8_FR`.

Server Installation and Configuration

This section provides step-by-step instructions on how to install and configure a JumpStart server and client running the Solaris 8 OE. Each step in configuring the server and client shows the commands and associated output. Explanations of the JumpStart configuration files and options are also provided. However, this section details *only* the fundamental JumpStart commands. All JumpStart information is provided to the JumpStart client through the use of a `sysidcfg` configuration file. For simplicity, this chapter does not use DHCP. Chapter 5, "Automating Installations," addresses the use of name services in the automation of JumpStart installations.

The scenario being detailed in this section consists of two systems: `server01` and `client01`. Both systems are connected to the same isolated network segment.

The `server01` system functions as the JumpStart boot server for `client01`. The `server01` system provides all the information for an automated JumpStart installation. This information includes the initial RARP, TFTP, `sysidcfg` file, begin scripts, Solaris OE packages, finish scripts, and any other information or scripts called by the begin and finish scripts.

Server Software Installation Steps

The first step in building a JumpStart server is to have the latest Solaris 8 OE installed. (Remember, the examples in this book are based on Solaris OE version 8 4/01.) Once the OE is installed, apply the latest patch cluster available from

SunSolve[sm] to the Solaris OE image of the server. It is assumed for this example that all required network configuration, account management, and any other tasks required to make the system functional have also been performed.

Once these tasks are performed, define a JumpStart partition with adequate space on the system. Given the size of Solaris OE images, you should set aside a partition of several gigabytes for the /jumpstart filesystem.

Installing Solaris OE Image

Copy any required Solaris OE image(s) into the /jumpstart/OS directory. Since the examples in this book are based on Solaris 8 OE 4/01, the directory is named Solaris_8_2001-04.

If you are using separate install and boot servers, you need to be aware that while the creation of a JumpStart install server changed with Solaris 8 OE, the installation of a JumpStart boot server *did not*.

To create a Solaris 8 OE JumpStart server, insert the first Solaris 8 OE software CD (labeled 1 of 2) into the CD-ROM drive and enter the following commands:

```
server01# pwd
/cdrom/sol_8_401_sparc/s0/Solaris_8/Tools
server01# ./setup_install_server /jumpstart/OS/Solaris_8_2001-04
```

The setup_install_server command produces the following output:

```
Verifying target directory...
Calculating the required disk space for the Solaris_8 product
Copying the CD image to disk...
Install Server setup complete
```

The first CD of the Solaris 8 OE is now installed. Insert the second CD (labeled 2 of 2) into the CD-ROM drive and enter the following command:

```
server01# pwd
/cdrom/sol_8_401_sparc_2/Solaris_8/Tools
server01# ./add_to_install_server /jumpstart/OS/Solaris_8_2001-04
```

The add_to_install_server command produces the following output:

```
The following Products will be copied to
/jumpstart/OS/Solairs_8_2001-04/Solaris_8/Product:

Solaris_2_of_2

If only a subset of products is needed enter Control-C
and invoke ./add_to_install_server with the -s option.

Checking required disk space...

Copying the Early Access products...
41990 blocks

Processing completed successfully.
```

This step completes the installation of the required Solaris OE software packages into the /jumpstart directory hierarchy. After the Solaris 8 OE software is installed on the JumpStart server, the /jumpstart directory must be made available to the JumpStart clients through the NFS® system. Add the following line to the /etc/dfs/dfstab file:

```
share -F nfs -o ro,anon=0 -d "Jumpstart Directory" /jumpstart
```

The options ro and anon=0 are required for JumpStart to function. See the share_nfs man page for additional details. Enter the following command to execute the share command:

```
server01# shareall
```

Note – If NFS services have not been started, you need to start them manually by executing the command /etc/init.d/nfs.server start before executing the shareall command.

Configuring the Client

Before the add_install_client command can be run, the JumpStart server, server01, must know the Ethernet address (MAC) and IP addresses of the JumpStart client(s). This information is provided to the JumpStart server through a name service—such as NIS+ or NIS—or through the use of the `/etc/hosts` and `/etc/ethers` files. The `add_install_client` JumpStart script uses this information to create an entry in the `/etc/bootparams` file. To simplify this example, we use the `/etc/ethers` and `/etc/hosts` files for this procedure.

Create an `/etc/ethers` file and add the following line:

```
8:0:20:82:d8:8f client01
```

Then, add the following line (for the JumpStart client) to the `/etc/hosts` file:

```
192.168.250.21 client01
```

When the JumpStart server receives the RARP request from the install client `client01`, it uses the client's Ethernet address to map an IP address to the client. The JumpStart server replies to the client specifying or telling its IP address.

Finally, add the JumpStart client, `client01`, to the JumpStart boot server with the following command:

```
server01# pwd
/jumpstart/OS/Solaris_8_2001-04/Solaris/Tools
server01# ./add_install_client -c server01:/jumpstart client01
sun4u
```

For additional details, see the `add_install_client` man page. This command produces the following output:

```
making /tftpboot
enabling tftp in /etc/inetd.conf
starting rarpd
starting bootparamd
starting nfsd's
starting nfs mount
updating /etc/bootparams
copying inetboot to /tftpboot
```

Note how the `add_install_client` command starts any services (which were not running before) required by the JumpStart server to function correctly. For example, if the NFS server on the JumpStart server isn't running, then it is started by the `add_install_client` command.

The JumpStart server, `server01`, is now configured to supply `client01` with an IP address and the Solaris OE. However, until a profile configuration file and `rules` file are created, the JumpStart server does not know what components of the Solaris OE to offer the client. Therefore, an automated JumpStart installation is not possible. Although an automated installation is *not* possible, an interactive Solaris installation can be performed at any time.

Automation of the Installation

Once the basic JumpStart components are installed, configure the JumpStart software so that it can automatically install the JumpStart client.

Configuring the `sysidcfg` file

To fully automate an installation, you must make available to the installation process all required information (that is, netmask, locale, timeserver, etc.). In this example, this information is provided through the `sysidcfg` configuration file. Additional information on how to implement automated JumpStart installations with other repositories, such as NIS+, NIS, DHCP, and files are detailed in Chapter 5, "Automating Installations."

The `add_install_client` command provides an option, -p, to specify the location of the `sysidcfg` file. This option directs the JumpStart client to use the `sysidcfg` file from the specified directory on the JumpStart server.

Place the following `sysidcfg` file in the `/jumpstart/Sysidcfg/Solaris_8` directory to fully automate the installation:

```
system_locale=en_US
timezone=US/Eastern
network_interface=primary {netmask=255.255.255.0
                           protocol_ipv6=no}
terminal=vt100
security_policy=NONE
root_password=DcwyMAx8TwtL2
name_service=NONE
timeserver=localhost
```

Note that the `sysidcfg` file contains keywords specific to the Solaris 8 OE (for example, `protocol_ipv6` and `security_policy`) and this file will not work with any previous Solaris OE versions. If an unrecognized keyword is encountered in the `sysidcfg` file, the installation reverts to an interactive installation and the entire `sysidcfg` file is ignored.

Note – All keywords in the `sysidcfg` file are explained in "`sysidcfg` File" on page 25 of Chapter 3.

Creating the `rules` File

JumpStart technology uses a `rules` file to specify how a JumpStart client is built *without* the use of interactive responses. The `rules` file is a text-based configuration file that contains a rule for each group of systems (or a single system) and contains information on configuring and installing the Solaris OE.

The `rules` file is created by a system administrator and contains the rules for all the different types of systems that are going to be installed in the environment. A `rules` file entry has five fields; the syntax of the `rules` files must follow this convention:

> *rule_keyword rule_value begin_script profile finish_script*

A `rules` file entry must specify at least a profile. In addition, begin and finish scripts can be included—they are executed by the JumpStart server before (or after) the Solaris OE is installed. If begin or finish scripts are not used, a minus character (–) must be used as a placeholder.

The following is a sample rule in a `rules` file:

```
hostname client01 - Profiles/basic.profile -
```

Note – Unless fully qualified path names are provided in the `rules` files, all paths are relative to the JumpStart server base directory. In the examples in this book, the JumpStart base directory is `/jumpstart`. This base directory is available to the begin and finish scripts run on the JumpStart client through the environment variable `SI_CONFIG_DIR`.

The examples in this chapter use only three of the five available fields in the `rules` file.

- `rule_keyword` — This field defines system attributes used in the `rule_value` to match a system with a corresponding value.

- `rule_value` — The value of this field is the corresponding value of the `rule_keyword`. The previous example uses this field to specify the host name of the system being installed.

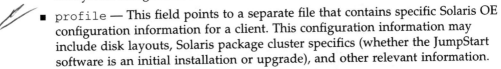

- `profile` — This field points to a separate file that contains specific Solaris OE configuration information for a client. This configuration information may include disk layouts, Solaris package cluster specifics (whether the JumpStart software is an initial installation or upgrade), and other relevant information.

Additional options are available in the `rules` file other than those described in this section. The section "`rules` File" on page 32 of Chapter 3, discusses these options in greater detail.

A basic `rules` file entry is used for the JumpStart environment described in this chapter. The any argument in the `rules` file is used for any JumpStart software installations when the JumpStart client has not matched any other rule in the `rules` file. If you add this entry to the `rules` file, all JumpStart clients defined on the server can be installed by this entry. To implement the any argument, create a `rules` file in the `/jumpstart` directory on the install server and include *only* the following entry:

```
any - - Profiles/basic.profile -
```

This entry is used in the `rules` file for the examples described throughout this chapter.

Creating the Profile

A `rules` file must specify a `profile`—this file defines how the Solaris OE system is installed and configured. The `profile` contains profile keywords and the corresponding value for each keyword. Each profile keyword defines a specific component of the Solaris OE installation and configuration process.

The following is the profile named `basic.profile` used in this chapter:

```
# install_type MUST be listed first
install_type    initial_install

# start with the minimal required number of packages
cluster         SUNWCuser

# define how the disk is laid out
partitioning    default
```

[handwritten note in left margin: This might be called of 1st something else on Solaris 10 filesys]

This example is a minimal profile. All profiles must contain *at least* the `install_type` keyword. The other keywords listed in the example are not required because they have default values that are used if *no* explicit definition is provided.

The `rules` file for this JumpStart environment uses the basic profile (`Profiles/basic.profile`) to define the components installed on the JumpStart client. Based on this profile, the following actions are performed:

1. `install_type initial_install` — A new Solaris OE is installed (as opposed to an upgrade).

2. `cluster SUNWCuser` — The Solaris OE cluster `SUNWCuser` is installed (including only the packages required for an End User installation). If this variable is not specified, the `SUNWCuser` cluster or End User cluster is installed by default.

3. `partitioning default` — If `default` is specified, the system configures the hard drive with Solaris OE defaults. If the `partitioning` keyword is *not* specified in the profile, the drive is partitioned *as if* `partitioning default` is specified.

By convention, all profiles should be stored in the `/jumpstart/Profiles` directory of the JumpStart install server. These files are grouped by system function. For example, systems that have similar functionality or requirements use the same profile. This standardization simplifies the installation process and streamlines system administration.

The elements used in the `basic.profile` are the most common elements used. Additional information on these specific elements is provided in "Profiles" on page 40 of Chapter 3.

Validating the `rules` File

The `rules` file and the profile require validation after creation or modification. They are validated by the `check` script, which creates a `rules.ok` file (if no errors are detected). The `check` script also verifies the existence of any specified begin or finish scripts. However, these scripts are not validated. The `rules.ok` file is used by the JumpStart server to install the Solaris OE. The `check` script is located on the JumpStart server in the directory `/jumpstart/OS/Solaris_8_2001-04/Solaris_8/Misc/jumpstart_sample`. This script must be copied to the base JumpStart directory of the JumpStart install server, `/jumpstart`, and then executed as follows:

```
server01# pwd
/jumpstart
server01# cp /jumpstart/OS/Solaris_8_2001-
04/Solaris_8/Misc/jumpstart_sample .
server01# ./check
```

This command generates the following output:

```
Validating rules...
Validating profile Profiles/basic.profile...
The custom JumpStart configuration is ok.
```

At this point the JumpStart client, `client01`, can be automatically installed. Start the automated installation by booting `client01` to the `ok` prompt and entering the following command:

```
ok> boot net - install
```

Note – The spaces around the minus character "-" are required for syntax. The reason for the spaces is explained in Chapter 9, "Customizing JumpStart Framework for Installation and Recovery."

Client Installation and Configuration

This section documents the messages generated from the console of the JumpStart client during JumpStart installation.

The initial JumpStart client boot messages (using the `sysidcfg` file) are as follows:

```
ok boot net - install
Resetting ...

Sun Ultra 1 SBus (UltraSPARC 167MHz), No Keyboard
OpenBoot 3.1, 128 MB memory installed, Serial #8575119.
Ethernet address 8:0:20:82:d8:8f, Host ID: 8082d88f.

Rebooting with command: boot net - install
Boot device: /sbus/ledma@e,8400010/le@e,8c00000 File and args: -
install
23e00
Booting the 32-bit OS ...

SunOS Release 5.8 Version Generic_108528-07 32-bit
Copyright 1983-2001 Sun Microsystems, Inc.  All rights reserved.
whoami: no domain name
Configuring /dev and /devices
Using RPC Bootparams for network configuration information.
Configured interface le0
Using sysid configuration file
10.0.0.20:/jumpstart/Solaris_8/sysidcfg
The system is coming up.  Please wait.
Starting remote procedure call (RPC) services: sysidns done.
Starting Solaris installation program...
Searching for JumpStart directory...
Using rules.ok from 10.0.0.20:/jumpstart.
Checking rules.ok file...
Using profile: Profiles/basic.profile
Executing JumpStart preinstall phase...
Searching for SolStart directory...
Checking rules.ok file...
Using begin script: install_begin
Using finish script: patch_finish
Executing SolStart preinstall phase...
Executing begin script "install_begin"...
Begin script install_begin execution completed.
```

Summary

This chapter presented details of how to configure and perform the required minimum components of an automated JumpStart installation. The components included:

- JumpStart server configuration
- Recommended server directory structure
- Server installation configuration

Additionally, the chapter discussed the basics of automating a Solaris OE installation, including configuration of the `sysidcfg` file, the `rules` file, and the profile. Finally, the chapter showed an example of an automated client installation.

## CHAPTER 3

JumpStart Customizations

Chapter 2, "JumpStart Overview," briefly touched on several key components of the JumpStart framework. This chapter examines these key components in depth, providing the information and recommendations necessary to best perform complex installations of the Solaris OE.

Additionally, this chapter details the techniques and mechanisms necessary to provide the basics of how to extend the JumpStart framework to best suit the needs of your datacenter.

This chapter describes the following topics and details the techniques to make the most of and extend the JumpStart framework:

- `sysidcfg` file
- Client definition
- `rules` file
- Profiles
- Scripting

`sysidcfg` File

The `sysidcfg` file is the mechanism used to *preconfigure* system configuration information to the client, enabling automated installations of the Solaris OE. Some configuration information, such as IPv6 and the root password, can only be preconfigured in the `sysidcfg` file. Other information can also be preconfigured in the `sysidcfg` file, depending on the name service used. For example, not all name services support the specification of a time zone. For automation of an installation, a name service, such as NIS+, can provide the time zone, but the time zone must be preconfigured in the `sysidcfg` if NIS is being used.

Examples of information that the `sysidcfg` file may contain are these data about the client:

- Time zone
- Root password

- Console device terminal type
- Network interface and options
- Name service used after installation

Keywords

The `sysidcfg` file specifies the configuration information as `keyword=value` pairs. For example, the following excerpt from a `sysidcfg` file configures the client's time zone to the MET time zone and the console device terminal type to be `vt100`.

```
timezone=MET
terminal=vt100
```

Time zone

Consult the contents of the directory /usr/share/lib/zoneinfo for a complete listing of time zones recognized by the Solaris OE. Keywords are placed in the `sysidcfg` file in any order. If a keyword is listed multiple times in a `sysidcfg` file, the value assigned at the first occurrence of the keyword is used.

These keywords are referred to as independent keywords, which designates them as a service or facility. Independent keywords are keywords that do not require a dependent keyword.

Dependent keywords specify additional configuration details that may be required by a service or facility. Dependent keywords are always associated with an independent keyword. Dependent keywords must follow the independent keyword they are associated with. Dependent keywords are enclosed in curly brackets ({ }). If there is more than one dependent keyword, they must be separated by a space. For example, to configure a client's network interface, specify the network interface device, the netmask, and whether IPv6 is used on that interface. The following portion of a `sysidcfg` file demonstrates the independent `sysidcfg` keyword (`network_interface`) and its dependent keywords (`netmask` and `protocol_ipv6`) to configure the client's primary network interface.

```
network_interface=hme0 {netmask=255.255.255.0 protocol_ipv6=no}
```

To achieve a completely automated installation of the Solaris OE, you must ensure that all client configuration information is available in a repository (or repositories) as the installation begins. The client configuration information is specified in the name service (NIS, NIS+, or DNS), in the `sysidcfg` file and local /etc files on the JumpStart server, or in a combination of these sources. In any case, the /etc/nsswitch.conf file on the JumpStart server must be correctly set to point to the correct configuration repositories being used.

Regardless of the repositories being used, it is important to note that if any configuration information cannot be found, the installation drops out of the automated installation and resorts to an interactive installation, prompting you for the missing information.

Note – Once the installation reverts to interactive, there is no way to return to an automatic installation.

For example, if a host named `timehost` is not found in the name service repository and the `sysidcfg` file does not have a timeserver entry, the automated installation fails and an interactive installation starts. To avoid an interactive installation, you must ensure that all configuration information is available to the client. This configuration information can be in the name service, the `sysidcfg` file, or a combination of the two.

However, if you need to troubleshoot problems, it is useful to pay close attention to the section where the installation reverts to an interactive installation. When the installation reverts to interactive, note the information that is first prompted for, the locale information (installation language, software language, or terminal type), system identification section (host name, IP address, or time), network configuration (name services, netmask, or IPv6 options), etc. These details can help you troubleshoot possible problems.

Name Services

Use the `sysidcfg` keyword `name_service` to specify the name service to which the installation client will *bind* after the installation completes. The possible values of `name_service` are:

- NIS+
- NIS
- LDAP
- DNS
- NONE

With the exception of NONE (which designates that the client is not configured to bind to any name service), the independent keyword `name_service` requires dependent keywords. These dependent keywords provide configuration information specific to the name service, for example, domain name, name servers, server search order, profile name, or profile location.

Note – LDAP client support is only available in the Solaris 8 OE 1/01 or later releases.

Keywords Specific to Intel Architecture

Four IA- platform-specific `sysidcfg` keywords address the hardware configuration needs of the Solaris OE for Intel Architecture (IA). These keywords designate the keyboard, graphics, and mouse devices:

- `keyboard`
- `monitor`
- `display`
- `pointer`

`sysidcfg` Keyword Listing

TABLE 3-1 describes the keywords you can use in the `sysidcfg` file.

TABLE 3-1   Keywords You Can Use in `sysidcfg`

Configuration Information	Platform	Keywords	Where to Find Values/Examples
Name service, domain name, name server	All	`name_service=NIS, NIS+, DNS, LDAP, NONE`	
		Options for NIS and NIS+: {domain_name=*domain_name* name_server=*hostname*(*ip_address*) netmask=*network_mask* }	`name_service=NIS` `{domain_name=blueprints.sun.com` `name_server=timber(10.0.1.1)}` `name_service=NIS+` `{domain_name=blueprints.sun.com` `name_server=timber(10.0.1.1)` `netmask=255.255.255.0}`
		Options for DNS: {domain_name=*domain_name* name_server=*ip_address*, *ip_address*, *ip_address* (three maximum) search=*domain_name*, *domain_name*, *domain_name*, *domain_name*, *domain_name*, *domain_name* (Six maximum, total length less than or equal to 250 characters)}	`name_service=DNS` `{domain_name=blueprints.sun.com` `name_server=10.0.1.10,10.0.1.20` `search=blueprints.sun.com,sun.com}` **NOTE:** Choose only one value for `name_service`. Include either, both, or neither of the `domain_name` and `name_server` keywords, as needed. If the `neither` keyword is used, omit the curly brackets {}.
		Options for LDAP: {domain_name=*domain_name* profile=*profile_name* profile_server=*ip_address*}	`name_service=LDAP` `{domain_name=blueprints.sun.com` `profile=default` `profile_server=10.0.1.1}`

TABLE 3-1 Keywords You Can Use in `sysidcfg` *(Continued)*

Configuration Information	Platform	Keywords	Where to Find Values/Examples
Network interface, host name, IP address, netmask, DHCP, IPv6	All	`network_interface=NONE,` `PRIMARY,` or *value* `{netmask=`*network_mask*`}`	`network_interface=primary` `{netmask=255.255.255.0}`
		If DHCP *is* used, specify: `{dhcp` `protocol_ipv6=`*yes_or_no*`}`	`network_interface=primary {dhcp` `protocol_ipv6=yes}`
		If DHCP is *not* used, specify: `{hostname=`*host_name* `default_route=`*ip_address* `ip_address=`*ip_address* `netmask=`*netmask* `protocol_ipv6=`*yes_or_no*`}`	`network_interface=le0` `{hostname=feron` `default_route=10.0.1.1` `ip_address=10.0.1.210` `netmask=255.255.255.0` `protocol_ipv6=no}`
			NOTE: Choose only one value for `network_interface`. Include any combination or none of the `hostname`, `ip_address`, and `netmask` keywords, as needed. If you do not use any of these keywords, omit the curly brackets ({}).
			NOTE: If DHCP is *not* used, you do not need to specify `protocol_ipv6` and `default_route`.
Root password	All	`root_password=`*root_password*	Encrypted password from `/etc/shadow`.
Security policy	All	`security_policy=kerberos,` `NONE` Options for Kerberos: `{default_realm=FQDN` `admin_server=FQDN` `kdc=FQDN1,FQDN2,FQDN3 }` Where `FQDN` is a fully qualified domain name.	`security_policy=kerberos` `{default_realm=blueprints.sun.COM` `admin_server=krbadmin.blueprints.s` `un.COM` `kdc=kdc1.blueprints.sun.COM,` `kdc2.blueprints.sun.COM}` **NOTE:** You can list a maximum of three key distribution centers (KDCs), but at least one is required.
Language in which to display the install program and desktop	All	`system_locale=`*locale*	The `/usr/lib/locale` directory or Appendix B, "Locale Values" of the *Solaris 8 Advanced Installation Guide* provides the valid locale values.

TABLE 3-1   Keywords You Can Use in `sysidcfg` *(Continued)*

Configuration Information	Platform	Keywords	Where to Find Values/Examples
Terminal type	All	`terminal=`*terminal_type*	The subdirectories in the `/usr/share/lib/terminfo` directory provide the valid terminal values.
Time zone	All	`timezone=`*timezone*	The directories and files in the `/usr/share/lib/zoneinfo` directory provide the valid time zone values.
			The time zone value is the name of the path relative to the `/usr/share/lib/zoneinfo` directory. For example, the time zone value for Mountain Standard Time in the United States is `US/Mountain`; the time zone value for Japan is `Japan`.
Date and time	All	`timeserver=localhost,` *hostname*`,`*ip_add*r	If you specify `localhost` as the time server, the system's time is assumed to be correct. If you specify the *hostname* or *ip_addr* (if you are not running a name service) of a system, that system's time is used to set the time.
Monitor type	IA	`monitor=`*monitor_type*	Run `kdmconfig -d` *filename*; append output to `sysidcfg` file.
Keyboard language, keyboard layout	IA	`keyboard=`*keyboard_language* `{layout=`*value*`}`	Run `kdmconfig -d` *filename*; append output to `sysidcfg` file.
Graphics card, screen size, color depth, display resolution	IA	`display=`*graphics_card* `{size=`*screen_size* `depth=`*color_depth* `  resolution=`*screen_resolution*`}`	Run `kdmconfig -d` *filename*; append output to `sysidcfg`.
Pointing device, number of buttons, IRQ level	IA	`pointer=`*pointing_device* `{nbuttons=`*number_buttons* `irq=`*value*`}`	Run `kdmconfig -d` *filename*; append output to `sysidcfg`.

`sysidcfg` File Example

The following example is a complete `sysidcfg` file that specifies that the installation is performed with the French locale (`system_locale=fr`). This means the installation messages are displayed in French. Additionally, the installation client's time zone is set to MET (France), the primary on-board network interface is preconfigured, the console terminal type is set to `vt100` for the installation, the security policy is set to `NONE` (Kerberos is not used), and the root password is set.

Finally, this `sysidcfg` file preconfigures the installation client to be an NIS client, and specifies that the system time information is to be obtained from the host with an IP address of 10.0.1.32.

```
system_locale=fr
timezone=MET
network_interface=primary {netmask=255.255.255.0
                           protocol_ipv6=no}
terminal=vt100
security_policy=NONE
root_password=Q8Sm16hItiff6
name_service=NIS        {domain_name=blueprints.sun.com
                         name_server=chevalnoir(10.0.1.16)
                         netmask=255.255.255.0}
timeserver=10.0.1.32
```

Client Definition

The `add_install_client` makes the installation client known to the JumpStart server. Further, the `add_install_client` command creates the necessary files and links on the JumpStart server to boot and install the client. The `add_install_client` command is located in the `Solaris_8/Tools` directory.

The `add_install_client` command requires that the client host name and architecture be specified. The `add_install_client` command creates the appropriate files and necessary links in the `/tftpboot` directory. The `add_install_client` then updates the `/etc/bootparams` file. The changes made to the `/etc/bootparams` file depend on the options specified. For example, to add the `UE220R` host `client01` as an installation client of `server01`, use the following command:

```
server01# cd /jumpstart/OS/Solaris_8_2001-04/Solaris_8/Tools
server01# ./add_install_client \
> -p server01:/jumpstart/Sysidcfg/Solaris_8/sysidcfg \
> -c server01:/jumpstart \
> client01 sun4u
```

Where:

- `-p` option specifies the directory containing the `sysidcfg` file to be used and creates the `sysid_config` identifier in the `/etc/bootparams` file.
- `-c` option specifies the JumpStart configuration directory to be used.

This is the location of the `rules.ok` file and is used as the value of the `SI_CONFIG_DIR` environment variable on the client during installation and sets the value of the root identifier of the `/etc/bootparams` file.

For additional information on the `add_install_client` command and the `/etc/bootparams` identifiers, consult the man pages for `add_install_client`(1M) and `bootparms`(4).

`rules` File

The `rules` file serves as a road map to the JumpStart installation. The `rules` file is a plain text (ASCII) file that provides an association between a host (or class of hosts) to be installed and the installation configuration and behaviors.

The `rules` file consists of rules, with each rule using a host selection criterion to map the installation client to a configuration profile, a begin script, and a finish script. The syntax of a rule is:

> *keyword value begin_script profile finish_script*

The *keyword value* pair is the selection criterion used to match a host to the installation behaviors. The *begin_script, profile,* and *finish_script* are the file names of the begin script, configuration profile, and finish script, respectively. At a minimum, a rule must consist of a keyword, its associated value, and a configuration profile. If a begin or finish script is not used, a minus character (-) must be used to designate this fact.

The rules are read sequentially, with the selection criterion used to find a match with the installation client information. It is possible that multiple selection criteria may match the installation client. If so, then the first rule encountered that matches the installation client is used. Use the # character to denote a comment in the `rules` file. Additionally, place the `rules` file in the top-level JumpStart directory.

The simplest keyword may be `hostname`, which matches *if* the host name specified as the value is the same as that of the installation client. For example, the following rule matches a system named `tympani` and does not use a begin script. However, the profile named `S8-server.profile` in the `Profiles` subdirectory and a finish script named `EE_Lab.fin` in the `Finish` subdirectory are used. For example:

```
hostname tympani \
        - \
        Profiles/S8-server.profile \
        Finish/EE_Lab.fin
```

You can negate any selection criteria by placing an `!` character in front of the keyword. The following example matches all hosts whose host name is not `tympani`.

```
!hostname tympani \
        - \
        Profiles/S8-server.profile \
        Finish/IntegrationTest.fin
```

Selection Criteria

The selection criteria provide the mechanism by which a client's installation request is associated with its installation behaviors. The JumpStart framework provides many selection criteria and enables you to define your own keywords. This section examines the most common or most interesting selection criteria and provides examples for defining and using your own selection criteria. For a complete listing of keywords and their associated values, consult the *Solaris 8 Advanced Installation Guide* (part number 806-0957-10) included with the Solaris 8 OE server distribution kit. The *Solaris 8 Advanced Installation Guide* is also available at `http://docs.sun.com`.

Client Architecture Keywords

There are several keywords that match in accordance with the kernel or processor architecture of the installation client. Use the `arch` keyword to match the client's processor architecture. The permissible values of `arch` are `sparc` for SPARC architecture-based systems or `i386` for IA-based systems. For example, the following rule matches any IA-based installation client.

```
arch i386 - Profiles/S8-IA.profile Finish/EE_Lab.fin
```

The second architecture-based keyword is `karch`; use it to match the client's kernel architecture. The valid values of `karch` are any of the currently supported Solaris OEs for SPARC kernel architectures, sun4u, sun4d, and sun4m, and the Solaris OE for IA kernel architecture, i386. The following rule matches any sun4u-based client.

```
karch sun4u \
        Begin/EE_Lab.beg \
        Profiles/S8-wrkgrpsvr.profile \
        Finish/EE_Lab.fin
```

Note – For versions 2.5.1 and 2.6 of the Solaris OE, the Ultra Enterprise™ 10000 kernel architecture is sun4u1. For versions 7 and higher of the Solaris OE, the Ultra Enterprise 10000 kernel architecture is sun4u.

The `model` keyword is similar to the `karch` keyword, but it allows a greater degree of control over matching an install client. The `model` keyword takes a value that specifies the name of the hardware implementation (that is, the output of the command `uname -i`). Following is an example of a rule to match an Ultra Enterprise server (Ultra Enterprise xx0 or Ultra Enterprise 10000) installation client with a kernel architecture of sun4u.

```
model SUNW,Ultra-Enterprise \
        Begin/dbcommon.beg \
        Profiles/S8-dbserver.profile \
        Finish/dbProduction.fin
```

The `model` keyword provides finer granularity for matching an installation client. For example, to match only an Ultra Enterprise 420R kernal architecture or an Ultra 80 installation client (which has a kernel architecture of sun4u) but no other sun4u architecture clients, the matching rule is:

```
model SUNW,Ultra-80 \
        Begin/dbcommon.beg \
        Profiles/S8-wrkgrpsvr.profile \
        Finish/dbIntegrationTest.fin
```

osname Keyword

Use the `osname` keyword to match the version of the Solaris OE currently installed on the installation client. The `osname` keyword takes a value specifying the clients currently installed on the version of the Solaris OE. This keyword is most useful when upgrading clients. For instance, use the following example to match any installation (or upgrade) client that currently has Solaris 2.6 OE installed.

```
osname Solaris_2.6 \
        Begin/dbupgrade.beg \
        Profiles/S8-wrkgrpsvr-upgrade.profile \
        Finish/dbIntegrationTest.fin
```

memsize Keyword

The `memsize` keyword matches according to the client's installed physical memory (RAM). The value specified must be in Mbytes and can be a single physical memory size or a range of memory sizes. For example, the following entry matches an install client with exactly 512 Mbytes of physical memory.

```
memsize 512 \
        Begin/dbcommon.beg \
        Profiles/S8-wrkgrpsvr.profile \
        Finish/dbIntegrationTest.fin
```

And this example matches any client with 1 Gbyte to 4 Gbytes of physical memory:

```
memsize 1024-4096 \
        Begin/dbcommon.beg \
        Profiles/S8-dbserver.profile \
        Finish/dbProduction.fin
```

disksize Keyword

The disksize keyword requires a value pair consisting of a disk device and a size range (specified in Mbytes). The installation client matches this rule if the client's specified disk falls within the specified range. This rule is very useful when you are installing clients with differing root disk geometries or sizes. Create configuration profiles specific for each disk size, and select each size at installation from the rules file. Configuration profiles are covered in depth in "Profiles" on page 40. In the following example, the first rule matches an installation client with a 9-Gbyte disk and uses the Profiles/S8-dbserver-9GBroot.profile profile to install the Solaris OE. The second rule matches an 18-Gbyte disk and uses the Profiles/S8-dbserver-18GBroot.profile profile.

```
disksize c0t0d0 8192-10240 \
        Begin/dbcommon.beg \
        Profiles/S8-dbserver-9GBroot.profile \
        Finish/dbProduction.fin
disksize c0t0d0 17408-194560 \
        Begin/dbcommon.beg \
        Profiles/S8-dbserver-18GBroot.profile \
        Finish/dbProduction.fin
```

Be careful when specifying the size range. A Mbyte is 1,048,576 bytes, and a disk labeled as 9 Gbytes is actually 9,000,000,000 bytes; 9,000,000,000 / 1,048,576 = 8,583 Mbytes, or approximately 8.5 Gbytes.

any Keyword

The any keyword has one required value, the minus character "-". This selection criteria matches any host and it should always be the last entry in the rules file. Use the any keyword this way:

```
any - - Profiles/S8-server.profile Finish/EE_Lab.fin
```

Combined Selection Criteria

You can combine selection criteria by using the && operator. This combined selection criterion is considered a match if all clauses of the conjunction match.

For example, consider the typical installation requirement of sizing the primary swap partition, based upon the amount of physical memory (RAM) in the system. Assume that the application requirements have been analyzed and were determined to be the following:

- 512 Mbytes of primary swap are required for systems having 256 Mbytes to 512 Mbytes of physical memory.

- 1 Gbyte of primary swap is required for systems having 512 Mbytes to 1 Gbyte of physical memory.

- 2 Gbytes of primary swap are required for systems with 1 Gbyte to 4 Gbytes of physical memory.

Also, assume that the following requirements are used to install the Solaris OE on clients that may have root disks of either 2 Gbytes, 9 Gbytes, or 18 Gbytes:

- 2-Gbyte disk means the / filesystem is 1 Gbyte.
- 9-Gbyte or 18-Gbyte disk means the / filesystem is 4 Gbytes.

The following rules implement these requirements, selecting the profile to partition the root disk with the appropriately sized swap and root filesystem:

```
# 256MB - 512MB memory, 2GB disk: 512MB swap, 1GB /
memsize 256-512 && disksize c0t0d0 1950-2048 \
        Begin/dbcommon.beg \
        Profiles/S8-dbserver-512MBswap-1GBroot.profile \
        Finish/dbProduction.fin
# 256MB - 512MB memory, 9GB - 18GB disk: 512MB swap, 4GB /
memsize 256-512 && disksize c0t0d0 8192-194560 \
        Begin/dbcommon.beg \
        Profiles/S8-dbserver-512MBswap-4GBroot.profile \
        Finish/dbProduction.fin
# 512MB - 1GB memory, 2GB disk: 1GB swap, 1GB /
memsize 512-1024 && disksize c0t0d0 1950-2048 \
        Begin/dbcommon.beg \
        Profiles/S8-dbserver-1GBswap-1GBroot.profile \
        Finish/dbProduction.fin
# 512MB - 1GB memory, 9GB - 18GB disk: 1GB swap, 4GB /
memsize 512-1024 && disksize c0t0d0 8192-194560 \
        Begin/dbcommon.beg \
        Profiles/S8-dbserver-1GBswap-4GBroot.profile \
        Finish/dbProduction.fin
# 1GB - 4GB memory, 9GB - 18GB disk: 2GB swap, 4GB /
memsize 1024-4096 && disksize c0t0d0 8192-194560 \
        Begin/dbcommon.beg \
        Profiles/S8-dbserver-2GBswap-4GBroot.profile \
        Finish/dbProduction.fin
```

Probes

All of the rules keywords, with the exception of any, have an equivalent probe keyword. Probe keywords do not take any values. Probe keywords extract information from the installation client and make that extracted information available to the begin and finish scripts in the form of shell environment variables. The name of the environment variable set by probe keywords is the name of the probe in all uppercase letters appended to SI_.

For example, when the memsize probe is encountered in a rules file, the value of the SI_MEMSIZE environment variable is set to the installation client's amount of physical memory; the karch probe sets the SI_KARCH environment variable to the installation client's kernel architecture. Because any of the begin or finish scripts may depend on environment variables set by probe keywords, the probe keywords are always placed at the beginning of the rules file.

The probe keyword `rootdisk` has no equivalent selection keyword. The `rootdisk` probe is used with the `disksize` or `installed` keywords and sets `SI_ROOTDISK` to the device currently defined as the root device. For example, the `rootdisk` probe is used with the `disksize rules` keyword:

```
disksize rootdisk 1450-2560 \
    - \
        Profiles/S8-dbserver-512MBswap-1GBroot.profile \
        Finish/dbProduction.fin
```

Creating Rule and Probe Keywords

In addition to the existing rule and probe keywords, custom keywords can be created. Create a custom keyword by supplying two Bourne shell functions. The first is a probe function that ascertains the desired information from the installation client and sets the corresponding `SI_` environment variable. The second required function is a comparison function that functions as the rule keyword. This function returns a 0 value if the keyword matches or a 1 value if the keyword does not match.

Consult the *Solaris 8 Advanced Installation Guide* for syntax and examples of creating custom keywords.

Validating the `rules` File

The installation process does not actually read the `rules` file; it reads the `rules.ok` file, a parsed and validated version of the `rules` file. After creating or making any modifications to the `rules` file, you must re-create the `rules.ok` file. You generate the `rules.ok` by executing the `check` script, found in the `Solaris_8/Misc/jumpstart_sample` subdirectory of the Solaris OE installation media. To ensure that all of the latest JumpStart features are available to your `rules` file and for ease of use, it is recommended that you copy the `check` script from the latest available version of the Solaris OE software CD to the `/jumpstart` directory.

```
server01# cp \
/cdrom/sol_8_401_sparc/s0/Solaris_8/Misc/jumpstart_sample/check \
/jumpstart
```

The following is an example of running the check script and generating a rules.ok file:

```
server01# pwd
/jumpstart
server01# ./check
Validating rules...
Validating profile Profiles/S8-server-FR.profile...
Validating profile Profiles/S8-wrkgrpsvr.profile...
The custom JumpStart configuration is ok.
server01# ls -al rules rules.ok
-rw-r--r--   1 root      other        326 Feb  5 11:12 rules
-rw-r--r--   1 root      other        278 Feb  5 11:18 rules.ok
```

For details and command-line options available on the check command, consult the check(1M) man page.

Profiles

As hinted in Chapter 2, "JumpStart Overview," the profile is a text file that serves as the road map for the installation of the Solaris OE to the installation client. Essentially, the profile contains all of the responses required by the Solaris OE installation program (suninstall). These responses are specified in the profile as keywords, one per line. Many profile keywords are available to control all aspects of the installation. You can find a complete list of the profile keywords in the *Solaris 8 Advanced Installation Guide* or at http://docs.sun.com. The remainder of this section examines the most powerful and most useful, but often overlooked, profile keywords.

Installation Types

The profile consists of profile keywords, one per line. Every profile must contain the install_type keyword, specifying whether this installation is an upgrade or a new installation. If the installation type is an upgrade and more than one root (/) filesystem on the installation client has an upgradable Solaris OE image on it, the profile must contain the root_device keyword to specify which root filesystem to upgrade. If any keywords are omitted, the Solaris OE installation default value or behavior is used. For example, if your profile does *not* specify an explicit partition for the root disk, the default Solaris OE partitioning is used.

System Types

The `system_type` keyword specifies what type of system is being ins
standalone server or a server for diskless clients. `standalone` is the d
since the use of diskless client workstations has become rare, `standalone` is the
recommended selection for this system type.

Package Clusters

For ease of reference and manipulation, the Solaris OE software packages are
organized into groups referred to as package clusters. Installation or deletion of a
package cluster is controlled by specification of the `cluster` keyword, followed by
the package cluster *group_name*, and an optional action (`add` or `delete`). If `add` or
`delete` is not specified, the default action is `add`. For example, the end-user
package cluster is specified by the following profile entry:

```
cluster SUNWCuser
```

The available package clusters and their associated `group_name` are:

- Core (`SUNWCreq`)
- End user (`SUNWCuser`)
- Developer (`SUNWCprog`)
- Entire distribution (`SUNWCall`)
- Entire distribution, with additional OEM support (`SUNWCXall`)

Other package clusters and package groupings are available; they are defined in the
`.clustertoc` file, which is found in the Solaris OE `Product` directory. For
example, in Solaris 8 OE 4/01 the `.clustertoc` file is located in the
`/cdrom/sol_8_401_sparc/s0/Solaris_8/Product` directory.

Specifying Optional Cluster Keyword Actions

The optional action of the cluster keyword can be specified during an initial
installation or an upgrade. However, the optional action is most useful during an
upgrade. When an upgrade is performed, the `add`/`delete` option functions are as
follows:

- Clusters currently installed are marked upgrade.

- `add` — If specified, the named package or cluster is installed during the upgrade
  (if not already installed on the system).

- `delete` — If specified, the named package or cluster (if already installed on the
  system) is deleted before the upgrade process begins.

Consider the need to upgrade a system currently installed with Solaris 2.6 and the SUNWCall package cluster to the Solaris 8 OE with only the SUNWCprog package cluster. Simply do an upgrade—the client is automatically upgraded to the Solaris 8 OE with the entire distribution. By use of the following profile entries, the Solaris 2.6 SUNWCall cluster is removed and then the OE is upgraded by installation of the SUNWCprog package cluster:

```
cluster SUNWCall delete
cluster SUNWCprog
```

Note – The sysidcfg root_password keyword is silently ignored when the Core software package cluster (SUNWCreq) is installed and no root password is present after the installation completes. The root_password keyword functions correctly for all other software package clusters. If you are performing Solaris OE minimization or operating system hardening with JumpStart technology, it is recommended that you install the SUNWCreq package cluster and set the root password with a finish script.

Adding/Deleting Packages to/from Clusters

Although the package clusters provide an easy way to reference and install a large number of packages, the granularity of package clusters is somewhat deficient. Consider the common task of installing the Solaris OE on a system used as a database server. Your analysis of the software requirements of the database application show that the entire Solaris distribution (SUNWCall) needs to be installed on the system to provide maximum application functionality to your users. However, since this system is used as a server, the desktop power management is not needed. Additionally, installation of the power management functions necessitates that you manually disable the power management functions after the installation.

The use of the profile keyword `package` allows the addition or deletion of individual software packages. By using `package` in conjunction with `cluster`, you can fine-tune the selection of the software packages to be installed. The following profile entries install the `SUNWCall` package cluster without the power management packages.

```
cluster      SUNWCall
package      SUNWpmr       delete
package      SUNWpmux      delete
package      SUNWpmu       delete
package      SUNWpmowm     delete
package      SUNWpmowr     delete
package      SUNWpmowu     delete
```

Note – The packages named in the `SUNWCreq` package cluster are required and cannot be deleted.

Partitioning Keywords and Disk Layout

One of the most common tasks in upgrading or installing the Solaris OE is the partitioning of the root disk, also referred to as the boot disk or system disk. This section examines the profile keywords for selecting and partitioning the root disk. However, the reasoning involved in choosing a root-disk-partitioning scheme and the relative merits of any scheme are outside the scope of this book. Readers interested in the topic of boot disk layout and partitioning should consult the information available on Sun BluePrints OnLine at `http://www.sun.com/blueprints`.

root_device Keyword

The `root_device` keyword specifies the disk used for the root disk and takes a single, required parameter in the Solaris OE $cXtYdZsN$ SCSI device naming notation:

```
root_device c0t0d0s0
```

The OpenBoot PROM™ (OBP) `boot-device` environment variable on the installation client is automatically updated to reflect the specified root device.

partitioning Keyword

Use the `partitioning` keyword to designate what method is to be used to partition the selected disk. Choose one of the following methods:

- `default` — Specifies that the Solaris OE default disk selection partitioning scheme is to be used. You can use a `filesys` keyword in the profile to modify the defaults.

- `existing` — Specifies that the existing Solaris OE filesystems (`/`, `/usr`, `/opt`, `/var`, and `/usr/openwin`) on the existing system disk are used. Any filesystems without Solaris OE (such as `/export/home`) are preserved.

- `explicit` — Indicates that the disk selection and partitioning information is specified in the `filesys` keyword.

filesys Keyword

Use the `filesys` keyword to specify the remote filesystems to be mounted and to partition and mount local filesystems. This section concentrates on the use of `filesys` for partitioning local disks only. Additionally, only a subset of the options for `filesys` are examined. For complete details on all options available with the `filesys` keyword, consult the *Solaris 8 Advanced Installation Guide*.

The format of the `filesys` keyword is:

```
filesys slice size [ filesystem optional_parameters ]
```

Where:

- *slice* specifies the disk selection and partitioning information and can be one of the following:
    - Keyword `any` — Instructs the installation program to install the Solaris OE on any one disk chosen at random. Use of this option is *not* recommended.
    - Solaris OE device specification — Specifies a disk on the installation client in the Solaris OE `cXtYdZsN` format (for example, `c0t0d0s0`). The installation process sets the OBP boot device environment variable, `boot-device`, to the specified device.
    - `rootdisk.sn` construct — Specifies the currently identified device as the boot disk used, with the `.sn` specifying the slice number on the disk to use.
- *size* can be specified with one of the following options:
    - *num* — Specifies the size of the filesystem by setting to *num* (in Mbytes).
    - `existing` — Uses the current size of the existing filesystem.

Note – When using this value, you can change the name of an existing slice by specifying *filesystem* as a different *mount_pt_name*.

- `auto` — Automatically determines the size of the filesystem depending on the selected software.
- `all` — The specified *slice* uses the entire disk for the filesystem. When you specify this value, no other filesystems can be placed on the specified disk.
- `free` — Uses the remaining unused (`free`) space on the disk for the filesystem.

  Note – If `free` is used as the value to `filesys`, it must be the last `filesys` entry in a profile.

- *start:size* — Explicitly partitions the filesystem: *start* is the cylinder where the slice begins; *size* is the number of cylinders for the slice.

- *filesystem* is optional and used when *slice* is specified as `any` or `cXtYdZsN`. If *filesystem* is not specified, `unnamed` is set by default, not allowing you to specify the *optional_parameters* value. Choose one of the following options:

  - *mount_pt_name* — Defines the filesystem's mount point name for example, `/var`.
  - `swap` — Uses the specified *slice* as `swap`.
  - `overlap` — Defines the specified *slice* as a representation of a disk region (VTOC value is `V_BACKUP`). By default, slice 2 is an overlap slice that is a representation of the whole disk.

    Note – You can specify `overlap` only when *size* is `existing`, `all`, or *start:size*.

  - `unnamed` — Defines the specified *slice* as a raw slice, so *slice* does not have a mount point name. If you do not specify *filesystem*, `unnamed` is used by default.
  - `ignore` — The specified *slice* is not used or recognized by JumpStart software. Use this option to ignore the specified filesystem on a disk during installation, so JumpStart software can create a new filesystem on the same disk with the same name. Use `ignore` only when `partitioning existing` is specified.

- *optional_parameters* can be one of the following options:

  - `preserve` — Preserves the filesystem on the specified *slice*.

    Note – `preserve` can be specified only when *size* is `existing` and *slice* is `cXtYdZsN`.

  - *mount_options* — Adds one or more mount options (same as the `-o` option of the `mount(1M)` command) to the `/etc/vfstab` entry for the specified *mount_pt_name*.

Note – If you need to specify more than one mount option, the mount options must be separated by commas and no spaces (for example, `ro,quota`).

Examples of `filesys` Specifications

The following `filesys` specification specifies the creation of `/u01`, a 4-Gbyte UFS filesystem on disk `c2t10d0s4` (an 18-Gbyte disk), starting at cylinder 0:

```
filesys c2t10d0s4 0:1784 /u01
```

To create an 8-Gbyte partition without a filesystem on `c4t12d0s1`, suitable for use as a raw partition for a database, use the following `filesys` specification:

```
filesys c4t12d0s1 8192 unnamed
```

Example of `filesys` Keyword Used with `Partitioning` Keyword

For maximum control over partitioning and root disk layout, use the `filesys` keyword in conjunction with the `partitioning` keyword. The following example demonstrates how these keywords are used together. This example designates the root disk to be a disk in a D1000 enclosure, `c2t8d0`, and partitions the root disk with an 8-Gbyte / filesystem on slice 0 and a 2-Gbyte swap partition on slice 1. The partition sizes are specified as a range of cylinders to control the placement of the partitions on the disk:

```
root_device c2t8d0
partitioning    explicit
filesys         rootdisk.s0 1453:7261 /
filesys         rootdisk.s1 1:1452 swap
```

The `filesys` size specification as *cylinder:size* permits exact placement of partitions on a disk. The cylinder specification, the number before the colon (:), specifies the starting cylinder for the partition. The size specification, the number after the colon (:), specifies the number of cylinders that the partition should occupy. In the previous example, the swap partition begins at cylinder 1 and is 1452 cylinders in size. The / filesystem begins at cylinder 1453 and extends to cylinder 8714 (1453 + 7261).

The swap partition is placed at cylinder 1 because the access to that area of a disk is typically faster. If the system needs to swap, this additional disk performance helps the overall system performance.

Other Useful Profile Keywords

The following miscellaneous profile keywords are useful for controlling the installation of localization packages and package cluster architectures.

`locale` Keyword

The system `locale` specifies how system information, such as messages, prompts, and errors, is communicated to the user. The `locale` controls the language and regional variances for a language, such as American English, British English, or Canadian English. The `locale` setting of the installation client is controlled by the `locale` keyword. Localization to Brazil would look like this example:

```
locale pt_BR
```

The default `locale` is set to American English (`en_US`). Consult the *Solaris 8 Advanced Installation Guide* for a complete listing of locales.

`geo` Keyword

The `geo` keyword specifies what regional locales (locale groupings) are installed on the system. It is important to note that the locales specified by the `geo` keyword are installed on the client; however, this does not change the current locale setting that is in effect for the Solaris OE installation currently running on the client (see the `locale` keyword in "sysidcfg File" on page 25). Multiple `geo` keywords can be specified. The following example installs the Western European and North American `locales` and sets the client's `locale` to European French.

```
geo W_Europe
geo N_America
locale fr
```

Consult the *Solaris 8 Advanced Installation Guide* for a complete listing of valid `geo` values and locales.

`isa_bits` Keyword

The `isa_bits` keyword specifies whether to install the 32- or 64-bit software packages. When any package cluster except the core cluster (`SUNWCreq`) is being installed, the default behavior is to install the 64-bit packages on sun4u architecture systems and the 32-bit packages on all other architectures. When SUNWCreq is being installed, the default behavior is to install the 32-bit packages regardless of the architecture. The isa_bits keyword is used to explicitly install the 64-bit SUNWCreq package cluster on sun4u architectures. For example,

```
cluster SUNWCreq
isa_bits 32
```

only installs the 32-bit packages.

Note – isa_bits is only available with the Solaris 8 OE or later, for the SPARC architecture.

Complete Profile Example

The following example is a complete profile used to install the entire distribution of the Solaris 8 OE on an Ultra Enterprise 420R kernal architecture, using a Sun StorEdge™ D1000 storage array as a boot device. Further, the system is installed with the Western European and North American regional locales and localized to the French locale.

```
install_type  initial_install
system_type   standalone
root_device   c2t8d0s0
partitioning  explicit
filesys       rootdisk.s0 1453:7261 /
filesys       rootdisk.s1 1:1452    swap
geo           W_Europe
geo           N_America
locale        fr
cluster       SUNWCall
package       SUNWpmux   delete  # Power Management binaries (64-bit)
package       SUNWpmu    delete  # Power Management binaries
package       SUNWpmr    delete  # Power Management config file&rc script
package       SUNWpmowr  delete  # Power Management OW Utilities, (Root)
package       SUNWpmowu  delete  # Power Management OW Utilities, (Usr)
package       SUNWpmowm  delete  # Power Management OW Utilities Man Pgs
```

The associated rules entry for the above example profile is:

```
model SUNW,Ultra-80 \
    - \
    Profiles/S8-wrkgrpsvr-fr.profile \
    Finish/EE_Lab.fin
```

Testing Profiles with pfinstall

Use the pfinstall command to test and validate the correctness of a profile before attempting to install a system. pfinstall can test a profile against the disk configuration on which pfinstall is being run (the -D option to pfinstall) or against a specified disk configuration (the -d disk-config-file option to pfinstall). You create a disk configuration with the prtvtoc command to write the disk geometry information to a file. Consult the pfinstall(1M) and prtvtoc(1M) man pages for details on creating a disk configuration file. The following is an example of running pfinstall with the previously created disk configuration file AllRootDisks.config:

```
server01# /usr/sbin/install.d/pfinstall \
> -d /jumpstart/AllRootDisks.config \
> -c /jumpstart/OS/Solaris_8_2001-04 \
> /jumpstart/Profiles/S8-wrkgrpsvr-fr.profile
```

For specific details on the pfinstall command syntax, consult the pfinstall man page. For, for an example of using pfinstall, see Chapter 4, "Postinstallation Procedures."

Scripting

The power and extensibility of the JumpStart framework comes from its scripting ability. The begin and finish scripts specified from the rules file enable the system administrator to customize the installation process and to automate complex, yet manageable and reproducible, system configurations.

Begin Scripts

A begin script is a Bourne shell script specified in the `rules` file that is executed *before* the Solaris OE installation begins. In the examples seen so far, a minus character (–) has been used to denote that a begin script is *not* to be executed. Begin scripts are not often used; the most common use of a begin script is to automatically back up a system before upgrading or installing a new Solaris OE on the client.

This example is `DumpToLocal.beg`: a begin script that performs a `ufsdump` of the root filesystem to a local tape device before starting an upgrade.

```
#!/bin/sh
ufsdump 0f /dev/rmt/0 /dev/dsk/${SI_ROOTDISK}
```

If the begin script generates any errors or messages, they are logged to the installation log. After installation, all logs are located on the installation client in the `/var/sadm/system/logs` directory. The log of any begin script execution output, warnings, or errors is `/var/sadm/system/logs/begin.log`. The associated `rules` entry specifying the `DumpToLocal.sh` begin script is as follows:

```
disksize rootdisk 1450-2560 \
    Begin/DumpToLocal.beg \
    Profiles/S8-dbserver-512MBswap-1GBroot.profile \
    Finish/dbProduction.fin
```

For an additional example of a begin script, see "Automating a StarFire™ Server Domain Installation" on page 51.

Finish Scripts

Like begin scripts, finish scripts are user-supplied Bourne shell scripts. Finish scripts are executed after the Solaris OE installation completes. Finish scripts provide a mechanism for system administrators to configure systems to their datacenter, departmental, or site standards. Further, finish scripts help ensure that all systems are consistently installed with little or no room for human error.

In its simplest form, use the finish script to copy configuration files on the installation client. The following example, `EE_Lab.fin`, shows a basic finish script used to back up the installation network configuration files (`/etc/hosts`, `/etc/netmasks`, and `/etc/resolv.conf`). The appropriate files and the `nsswitch.conf` file (specifying DNS, used for host name resolution) are then copied from the `$SI_CONFIG_DIR/Files` (`/jumpstart/Files`) directory of the JumpStart server to the installation client's `/etc` directory. A standard `.profile` for the `root` user is then copied to `/.profile`.

```
#!/bin/sh
# EE_Lab.fin
# Finish script for default EE_Lab setup
#
# No additions to /etc/passwd and /etc/system are required.
# Assumes the root password was set in sysidcfg#
#
echo "Creating hosts, netmasks, ntp.conf, "
echo "resolv.conf and nsswitch.conf... "
cp /a/etc/inet/hosts        /a/etc/inet/hosts.fcs
cp /a/etc/inet/netmasks    /a/etc/inet/netmasks.fcs
cp ${SI_CONFIG_DIR}/Files/EE_Lab.hosts /a/etc/inet/hosts
cp ${SI_CONFIG_DIR}/Files/EE_Lab.netmasks /a/etc/inet/netmasks
cp ${SI_CONFIG_DIR}/Files/EE_Lab.resolv.conf /a/etc/resolv.conf
cp ${SI_CONFIG_DIR}/Files/EE_Lab.nsswitch.conf /a/etc/nsswitch.conf
#
# Copying template for root .profile
#
echo "Creating /a/.profile..."
cp ${SI_CONFIG_DIR}/Files/slash.profile /a/.profile
```

Note that the installation directory (`/jumpstart`, in this example) is an NFS system mounted from the JumpStart server to `$SI_CONFIG_DIR` on the installation client. Additionally, the installation procedure has the disk device mounted on `/a`. During the installation, the disk the OE is being installed to is mounted on `/a`. Additionally, `/jumpstart`, the JumpStart configuration directory specified by the `-c` option to `add_install_client`, is mounted, and the environment variable `SI_CONFIG_DIR` is automatically set to its mount point.

See Chapter 10, "Solaris Security Toolkit," for additional examples of finish scripts.

Automating a StarFire™ Server Domain Installation

Another example to consider is the use of a JumpStart server to install an Ultra Enterprise 10000 (StarFire) server domain. A Ultra Enterprise 10000 server domain is installed as any other Solaris OE system. However, a Ultra Enterprise 10000 server domain requires information about the System Service Processor (SSP) responsible for managing and monitoring that domain. This required SSP information must be stored in the files `/etc/ssphostname` and `/etc/ssphostaddr` on the domain, and these files must be created during installation of the domain. If the SSP configuration information necessary to populate these files is not present during the installation, the installation becomes interactive and prompts for the required SSP information.

The rudiments of automating this procedure are in the Solaris OE installation media. The supplied finish script, `install_config`, located under the Solaris OE media directory of the CD-ROM or on the JumpStart server (in this example, `/jumpstart/OS/Solaris_8_2001-04/Solaris_8/Tools/Boot/usr/sbin/install.d/install_config`) contains a finish script that can be used. The following technique explains how you provide this SSP information with a begin script and the supplied finish script to fully automate a StarFire server domain JumpStart software installation.

For all installations, whether they are from CD-ROM or a JumpStart server, the installation procedures use a secondary `rules.ok` file and rudimentary begin and finish scripts. The prompting for SSP information is controlled from this secondary `rules.ok` file located in the `./tools/Boot/usr/sbin/install.d/install_config` directory, under the Solaris OE media directory on the JumpStart server or Solaris OE installation CD media.

To automate the installation of a StarFire domain, you can have a begin script temporarily store the required SSP information on the installation client's `/tmp` directory before the installation begins. The information is then accessed by a finish script after installation completes; this finish script creates the necessary SSP information files on the domain being installed.

The following begin script, `Begin/set_SSP.beg`, saves the SSP host name and IP address for use by the finish script, `Finish/set_SSP.fin`. For simplicity, these values are hardcoded. You may want to have a more general method of providing or locating this information in the begin script.

```
#!/bin/sh
#
# set_SSP.beg
# Save SSP information on installation client for
# later use by set_SSP.fin
#
TMPSSPHOSTNAME=/tmp/ssphostname
TMPSSPHOSTADDR=/tmp/ssphostaddr
#
# The SSP's hostname is saved in this file
echo chips1 > ${TMPSSPHOSTNAME}
# the SSP's IP address is saved in this file
echo 10.0.1.64 > ${TMPSSPHOSTADDR}
```

The supplied finish script from the
`../Solaris_8/Tools/Boot/usr/sbin/install.d/install_config` can now
be used, unmodified, to reference the information stored by the begin script. The
supplied finish script is copied to the `/jumpstart/Finish` directory.

```
server01# cp /jumpstart/OS/Solaris_8_2001-
04/Solaris_8/Tools/Boot/usr/sbin/install.d/install_config/ssp_fi
nish /jumpstart/Finish/set_SSP.fin
```

Assuming the domain to be installed is named `ponch` or `jon`, a simple but
appropriate `rules` file entry is:

```
hostname ponch \
        Begin/set_SSP.beg \
        Profiles/S8-dbserver-18GBroot.profile \
        Finish/set_SSP.fin
hostname jon \
        Begin/set_SSP.beg \
        Profiles/S8-dbserver-18GBroot.profile \
        Finish/set_SSP.fin
```

Additional techniques for accomplishing postinstallation tasks such as automated
patch and package installation are covered in Chapter 4, "Postinstallation
Procedures."

Driver Scripts

By writing the begin and finish scripts in a modular fashion and having each script do one well-defined task, you can easily chain the scripts together. To control execution of multiple begin or finish scripts, it is recommended that you use a driver script. The driver should be minimal, providing error checking and management of the environment before executing the specified scripts.

The following example shows EE_LabStarFire.driver, a basic driver that iterates over a list of finish scripts (SCRIPT_LIST), executing each of them in turn. This driver executes both finish scripts shown in the two previous examples in "Finish Scripts" on page 50 and in "Automating a StarFire™ Server Domain Installation" on page 51, EE_Lab.fin and set_SSP.fin:

```
#!/bin/sh
#
# Basic driver for Enterprise Engineering lab StarFire hosts.
#
FINISH_DIR="${SI_CONFIG_DIR}/Finish"
SCRIPT_LIST="EE_Lab.fin set_SSP.fin"

for script in ${SCRIPT_LIST}
do
    if [ -f "${FINISH_DIR}/${script}" ]; then
        echo "Starting finish script: ${script}"
        echo ""
        . ${FINISH_DIR}/${script}
    else
        echo "ERROR: File not found: ${script}"
    fi
done
```

The rules entry used for this example looks similar to the following:

```
hostname ponch \
        Begin/set_SSP.beg /
        Profiles/S8-dbserver-18GBroot.profile \
        Finish/EE_LabStarFire.driver
hostname jon \
        Begin/set_SSP.beg /
        Profiles/S8-dbserver-18GBroot.profile \
        Finish/EE_LabStarFire.driver
```

See Chapter 10, "Solaris Security Toolkit," for additional examples of driver scripts used to secure and harden the Solaris OE.

Summary

In this chapter we looked at the major components of the JumpStart framework. We saw how the `sysidcfg` file is used to provide preconfiguration information to the client and examined the keywords necessary for automating installations. Armed with such information, you should be able to fully automate the installation of the Solaris OE.

We learned that the `rules` file controls and selects installation behaviors. We examined the `rules` keywords and techniques for combining the selection criteria Details of the probe keywords, customization, and the writing of custom rules added to the appreciation of rules.

The chapter then turned to the actual installation of the Solaris OE, describing the installation profile and the more useful profile keywords for automating and controlling the installation. Additionally, we saw how to use profile keywords to partition the root disk and localize system software.

Finally, we examined the scripting mechanisms of the JumpStart framework: the begin and finish scripts, and the use of a driver script to combine finish script modules. Additionally, we learned of a technique for automating a StarFire server domain installation through the use of a begin script in conjunction with a finish script.

## CHAPTER 4

Postinstallation Procedures

Automating and standardizing the installation of the Solaris Operating Environment (Solaris OE) along with the associated unbundled software products and datacenter management tools are two of the largest challenges facing system administrators. This chapter builds on the advanced JumpStart technology techniques presented in Chapter 3, "JumpStart Customizations." It examines some of the lesser-known (but more powerful) configuration options of the JumpStart application to perform a site-standard, hands-free installation of the Solaris OE and a hands-free installation of unbundled software applications, such as VERITAS Volume Manager (VxVM), and software patches. This chapter describes the following topics and techniques:

- Package installation challenges
- Automation of patch installation
- Automation of interactive package installation
- Automatic interactive configuration

Note – While this chapter presents several techniques for automated installation of software packages, be aware that not all software applications can be automatically configured during installation.

Note – To present complete examples of finish scripts and the corresponding JumpStart configuration files, we repeat in this chapter some information from previous chapters.

Package Installation Challenges

It is important to note that not all software or patches are correctly packaged to allow installation from the miniroot. These problematical packages usually fall into three broad categories:

1. Patch installation patches and some packages that do not correctly relocate all or some of their components under /a, the root mount point of the system being installed.

2. Packages that require interactive installation.

   The AnswerBook™ software and similar packages usually fall into this category since they attempt to interact with the user during installation to determine, for example, the type of AnswerBook software installation to be done (Heavy or nil) and the directory location in which the AnswerBook software should be placed.

3. Packages that require interactive configuration.

   VxVM encapsulation of the boot disk is an example. Some packages require interactive configuration after the package has been installed.

This chapter presents example finish scripts that provide solutions for patches or products in each of these three areas. These finish scripts and techniques enable the system administrator to automate the installation of: patches and unbundled software packages.

Additionally, techniques for postinstallation configuration of unbundled software are presented.

Note – For clarity in this chapter's examples, we do not use a driver script. A driver script is recommended, though, for production use and ease of maintenance.

Throughout the examples in this chapter, the following host names are used:

Host Name	Function
server01	JumpStart server
client03	Install client

Additionally, name services are not used; rather, the /etc files and sysidcfg file on server01 provide name resolution and system identification information.

Caution – Since this chapter presents several scripts and procedures, it is important to keep in mind that these scripts are not *production ready*. These scripts are presented to demonstrate a technique only, so the scripts contain limited or no error checking.

Software Package Utilities

To automate software package installation, the finish scripts examined in this chapter make extensive use of the `pkgask` and `pkgadd` commands. Essentially, `pkgask` examines the specified software package and extracts the prompts or questions used by `pkadd` during the package installation. `pkgask` then uses those package installation questions, storing the responses in the specified file. This file of stored responses to the package installation questions is referred to as the response file. Complete details on these commands and the use of response files can be found on the `pkgask(1M)` and `pkgadd(1M)` man pages.

An additional software package facility that the following finish scripts use is the `noask` package administration file. The `noask` package administration file avoids interactive package installation by instructing the `pkgadd` command to use its defaults or to bypass checks, such as the check for adequate disk space. The use of an administration file is documented on the `pkgadd` man page (the `-a` option), and the `noask` file is also documented in the *Solaris System Administration Guide, Volume 1* available at `http://docs.sun.com`.

The `noask` file used in all examples in this chapter is shown below:

```
mail=
instance=overwrite
partial=nocheck
runlevel=nocheck
idepend=nocheck
rdepend=nocheck
space=nocheck
setuid=nocheck
conflict=nocheck
action=nocheck
basedir=default
```

Automation of Patch Installation

Solaris OE patches are installed individually with the `patchadd` command or, with older versions of the Solaris OE, as a patch cluster with the `install_cluster` script. The `install_cluster` script iterates over the list of patches to be installed, essentially doing the equivalent of a `patchadd` on each of the specified patches. Depending on the patch being installed (and the facility or services it is patching), `patchadd` may require varying levels of services to be up and configured in order to successfully complete installation of the patch. For example, the Solaris 8 OE `sort` facility relies on the loopback filesystem. Because `patchadd` uses the `sort` facility for several patches (such as patch 109783, the `nfsd` patch), the availability of the loopback filesystem is necessary for successful installation of many patches.

The following finish script, `install-recommended-patches.fin`, detects the version of the Solaris OE being installed and installs the corresponding patch cluster from under the `/jumpstart/Patches` directory.

The script installs all the patches by using the `chroot` command, setting the root directory to `/a` (the mount point for the newly installed Solaris OE), and then executing the `install_cluster` or `patchadd` command as appropriate.

Some patches do not correctly install with `chroot` unless the loopback filesystem (`lofs`) and the mounted filesystem table (`/etc/mnttab`) are available. This script starts `lofs` on the miniroot by making a loopback mount of `/proc` and copying `/etc/mnttab` from the miniroot before beginning the patch installation.

```
#
# This script is responsible for installing a Sun Recommended
# and Security Patch Cluster from ${BASEDIR}/${PATCH_DIR}.

errorCondition=0
mountedProc=0

BASEDIR="/a"
PATCH_SERV_DIR=""
PATCH_DIR="/mnt"
MNTTAB="${BASEDIR}/etc/mnttab"
OE_VER="'uname -r'"

mount -F nfs -o ro server01:/jumpstart/Patches \
        ${BASEDIR}/${PATCH_DIR}

case ${OE_VER} in

    5.8)
        PATCH_SERV_DIR=8_Recommended
        ;;

    5.7)
        PATCH_SERV_DIR=7_Recommended
        ;;

    5.6)
        PATCH_SERV_DIR=2.6_Recommended
        ;;

    5.5.1)
        PATCH_SERV_DIR=2.5.1_Recommended
        ;;

    *)
        errorCondition=1
        ;;

esac
if [ ${errorCondition} = 0 ]; then
    if [ ! -d ${BASEDIR}/${PATCH_DIR} ]; then
```
(continued next page)

```
(continued from previous page)
        echo "The directory, ${PATCH_DIR}, does not exist."
    else
        # Some patches require the procfs filesystem be used when
        # installing using chroot.
        if [ -d /proc ]; then
            if [ "'df -n /proc | awk '{ print $3 }''" = "proc" ]; then
                if [ -d ${BASEDIR}/proc ]; then
                    if [ "'df -n ${BASEDIR}/proc | \
                        awk '{ print $3 }''" != "proc" ]; then
                        mount -F lofs /proc ${BASEDIR}/proc
                        mountedProc=1
                    fi
                fi
            fi
        fi

        if [ ! -s ${MNTTAB} ]; then
            if [ -s /etc/mnttab ]; then

                # First create ${MNTTAB} so patches can read it:

                echo "Copying /etc/mnttab from miniroot to ${MNTTAB}"
                echo ""
                rm -f ${MNTTAB}

                if [ "${OE_VER}" = "5.5.1" ]; then

                    # This is necessary for "install_cluster" to get the mount
                    # point for /var/sadm/patch from the "real" root filesystem.

                    cat /etc/mnttab | sed 's/\/a/\//g' > ${MNTTAB}

                    # This is necessary for "df" to execute which is needed by
                    # "install_cluster" to determine if enough free disk
                    # space exists on the target system.

                    touch           ${BASEDIR}/etc/.mnttab.lock
                    chown root:root ${BASEDIR}/etc/.mnttab.lock
                    chmod 644       ${BASEDIR}/etc/.mnttab.lock
                else
                    cp /etc/mnttab ${MNTTAB}
                fi
(continued next page)
```

```
(continued from previous page)
        else
            echo "Could not find a valid /etc/mnttab"
            errorCondition=1
        fi
    fi
if [ ${errorCondition} = 0 ]; then

        SHOWCOMMAND=""

        if [ -x ${BASEDIR}/usr/sbin/patchadd ]; then
            SHOWCOMMAND="/usr/sbin/patchadd"
        elif [ -x ${BASEDIR}/usr/bin/showrev ]; then
            SHOWCOMMAND="/usr/bin/showrev"
        fi

        cd ${BASEDIR}/${PATCH_DIR}

        if [ -d ${PATCH_SERV_DIR} ]; then
            echo "Installing the ${PATCH_SERV_DIR} patch cluster."
            echo ""

            if [ "${SHOWCOMMAND}" = "/usr/sbin/patchadd" ]; then
                chroot ${BASEDIR} /usr/sbin/patchadd -d -u \
                    -M ${PATCH_DIR}/${PATCH_SERV_DIR} patch_order
            elif [ -x ${PATCH_DIR}/${PATCH_SERV_DIR}/install_cluster ]; then
                chroot ${BASEDIR} \
                    ${PATCH_DIR}/${PATCH_SERV_DIR}/install_cluster -q \
                    ${PATCH_DIR}/${PATCH_SERV_DIR}
            else
                echo "Cannot find /usr/sbin/patchadd or install_cluster"
            fi
        else
            echo "Could not find the ${PATCH_SERV_DIR} patch cluster"
        fi
    fi

    umount ${BASEDIR}/${PATCH_DIR}
    if [ ${mountedProc} = 1 ]; then
        umount ${BASEDIR}/proc
    fi
    fi
fi
```

Automation of Interactive Package Installation

It is important to note that if any information is missing from the repository, the installation drops out of the automated installation and resorts to an interactive installation, prompting you for the missing information. Once an interactive installation is resorted to, there is no way to return to an automated installation. For example, if a host named `timehost` is not found in the name service repository and the `sysidcfg` file does not have a `timeserver` entry, the automated installation fails and an interactive installation starts. You are first presented with two screens of introductory information and then prompted for the correct time. After you supply the correct time, the installation continues as an interactive installation.

By always providing all required keywords in the `sysidcfg` file, you can completely avoid this problem. However, if you need to troubleshoot problems such as this, it is useful to pay close attention to the section where the installation reverts to an interactive installation—what information is first prompted for, the locale information (installation language, software language, or terminal type), system identification section (host name, IP address, or time), network configuration (name services, netmask, or IPv6 options), etc.

Following is an example of the procedures and finish script which effect an automated installation of the Solaris 8 OE and VxVM 3.0.4. You can see that `client03` is installed with the Solaris 8 OE 4/01 and VxVM 3.0.4. Note that VxVM is installed but not configured. The automatic encapsulation of the boot disk is covered in "Automatic Interactive Configuration" on page 73.

1. **Configure** `server01` **as a JumpStart server.**

```
server01# share -F nfs -o ro,anon=0 /jumpstart
server01# mkdir /jumpstart/OS/Solaris_8_2001-04
server01# cd /cdrom/sol_8_401_sparc/s0/Solaris_8/Tools
server01# ./setup_install_server \
> /jumpstart/OS/Solaris_8_2001-04
Verifying target directory...
Calculating the required disk space for the Solaris_8 product
Copying the CD image to disk...
Install Server setup complete
[ insert Solaris 8 Software cd 2 of 2 ]
server01# cd /cdrom/sol_8_401_sparc_2/Solaris_8/Tools
server01# ./add_to_install_server \
> /jumpstart/OS/Solaris_8_2001-04

The following Products will be copied to
/jumpstart/OS/Solaris_8_2001-04/Solaris_8/Product:

Solaris_2_of_2

If only a subset of products is needed enter Control-C
and invoke ./add_to_install_server with the -s option.

Checking required disk space...

Copying the Early Access products...
213481 blocks


Processing completed successfully.
```

2. **Add the VxVM packages into the JumpStart server tree on** `server01`.

```
server01# cd /cdrom/volumne_manager_3_0_4_solaris
server01# find . -print |cpio -pudm \
/jumpstart/Packages/vxvm_3.0.4
```

3. **Add** `client03` **as an install client of** `server01`. **Specify that the** `/etc/hosts` **file is to be updated with the IP address and Ethernet MAC address of the client being added (the** `-i` **and** `-e` **options to** `add_install_client`, **respectively), the**

directory containing the `sysidcfg` file (the -p option to `add_install_client`), and the JumpStart configuration directory (the -c option to `add_install_client`).

```
server01# cd /jumpstart/OS/Solaris_8_2001-04/Solaris_8/Tools
server01#./add_install_client \
> -i 10.1.1.6 -e 8:0:20:7c:ff:d0 \
> -p server01:/jumpstart/Sysidcfg/Solaris_8 \
> -c server01:/jumpstart \
> client03 \
> sun4u
```

4. **Verify the contents of** /etc/bootparams.

```
server01# cat /etc/bootparams
client03   root=server01:/jumpstart/OS/Solaris_8_2001-
04/Solaris_8/Tools/Boot
install=server01:/jumpstart/OS/Solaris_8_2001-04 boottype=:in
sysid_config=server01:/jumpstart/Sysidcfg/Solaris_8
install_config=server01:/jumpstart rootopts=:rsize=32768
```

5. **Create or modify** sysidcfg.

To have an automated installation, you must ensure that all client configuration information is available to the client installation program at boot. The configuration information can be made available from an NIS+ server, an NIS server, the sysidcfg file, or by any combination of these sources.

```
server01# cd /jumpstart/Sysidcfg/Solaris_8
server01# cat sysidcfg
system_locale=en_US
timezone=US/Pacific
network_interface=primary {netmask=255.255.255.0
                           protocol_ipv6=no}
terminal=xterm
security_policy=NONE
name_service=NONE
timeserver=server01
root_password=P.YSjsh8A4Rbg
```

6. **Create the installation profile**. Note the following: the standard Solaris 8 OE partitioning scheme is used, / is installed on `slice 0`, and swap is installed on `slice 1`. Note further, though, that `swap` occupies cylinders 1 through 690, and / occupies cylinders 691 through 2730.

This profile installs the entire Solaris OE cluster (SUNWCall), with the exception of the power management utilities.

```
server01# cd /jumpstart/Profiles
server01# cat S8-server.profile
install_type      initial_install
system_type       standalone
root_device       c0t0d0
partitioning      explicit
filesys           c0t0d0s0        691:2040        /
filesys           c0t0d0s1        1:690           swap
cluster           SUNWCall
package SUNWpmowm          delete
package SUNWpmowr          delete
package SUNWpmowu          delete
package SUNWpmr            delete
package SUNWpmu            delete
package SUNWpmux           delete
server01# /usr/sbin/install.d/pfinstall -D \
> -c /jumpstart/OS/Solaris_8_2001-04 \
> S8-server.profile
```

The `pfinstall` command in the preceding example is used to verify the correctness of the profile before the installation process begins. See the `pfinstall`(1M) command man page for additional details.

7. **Use** `pkgask(1)` **to create the response files for automating the installation of the VERITAS VRTSvmdoc and VRTSvmsa packages.**

Installation of the VRTSvmdoc (user documentation) and VRTSvmsa (graphical user interface) packages prompts for location and configuration information. The use of a response file allows installation of these packages to be automated.

```
server01# pkgask -r /jumpstart/Packages/VRTSvmdoc.response \
> -d /jumpstart/Packages/vxvm_3.0.4/pkgs VRTSvmdoc

Processing package instance <VRTSvmdoc> from
</jumpstart/Packages/vxvm_3.0.4/pkgs>

VERITAS Volume Manager (user documentation)
(sparc) 3.0.4,REV=04.18.2000.10.00

   1   PostScript
   2   PDF

Select the document formats to be installed (default: all) [?,??,q]: all
[PostScript] [PDF] will be installed.

Response file </jumpstart/Packages/VRTSvmdoc.response> was created.

Processing of request script was successful.
server01# pkgask -r /jumpstart/Packages/VRTSvmsa.response \
> -d /jumpstart/Packages/vxvm_3.0.4/pkgs VRTSvmsa

Processing package instance <VRTSvmsa> from
</jumpstart/Packages/vxvm_3.0.4/pkgs>

VERITAS Volume Manager Storage Administrator
(sparc) 3.0.6,REV=04.03.2000.14.30

Where should this package be installed? (default: /opt]) [?,q] /opt

Should the Apache HTTPD (Web Server) included in this package be
installed?
(default: n) [y,n,?,q] n

Should the Volume Manager Storage Administrator Server be installed on
this system?
(The Volume Manager Storage Administrator Client will be installed
regardless)
(default: y) [y,n,?,q] y

Response file </jumpstart/Packages/VRTSvmsa.response> was created.
(continued next page)
```

```
(continued from previous page)
Processing of request script was successful.
server01# pkgask -r /jumpstart/Packages/S8-VRTSvxvm.response \
> -d /jumpstart/Packages/vxvm_3.0.4/pkgs VRTSvxvm

Processing package instance <VRTSvxvm> from
</jumpstart/Packages/vxvm_3.0.4/pkgs>

VERITAS Volume Manager, Binaries
(sparc) 3.0.4,REV=04.18.2000.10.00

This package, VxVM 3.0.4, is supported on Solaris 2.5.1, 2.6,
7, and 8.  You appear to be running Solaris 8.  Press
ENTER to install VxVM 3.0.4 for Solaris 8, or enter
another Solaris version number if you are certain that you want to
install the drivers for a different release of Solaris.

Install for which version of Solaris?
[8, 7, 2.6, 2.5.1] (default: 8): 8
Installing VxVM for Solaris 8

The following Sun patch(s) are required for Solaris 8.
Sun patch(s):


Continue installation? [y,n,q,?] (default: n): y


Response file </var/tmp/S8-VRTSvxvm.response> was created.

Processing of request script was successful.
server01# cat /jumpstart/Packages/VRTSvmdoc.response
CLASSES=PostScript PDF
server01# cat /jumpstart/Packages/VRTSvmsa.response
BASEDIR=/opt
CLIENT_BASEDIR=/opt
CLASSES= jre cliserv server client
URL=
server01# cat /jumpstart/Packages/S8-VRTSvxvm.response
REQ_OS_VERS=5.8
```

8. Create the finish script.

```
server01# cat /jumpstart/Packages/install-S8-vxvm304.fin
#!/bin/sh

BASEDIR=/a
VXPRODUCT=${SI_CONFIG_DIR}/Packages/vxvm_3.0.4/pkgs

echo "Installing VRTSvxvm..."
pkgadd -a ${SI_CONFIG_DIR}/Packages/noask \
-r ${SI_CONFIG_DIR}/Packages/S8-VRTSvxvm.response \
-d ${VXPRODUCT} \
-R ${BASEDIR} VRTSvxvm
#
echo "Installing VRTSvmsa..."
pkgadd -a ${SI_CONFIG_DIR}/Packages/noask \
-r ${SI_CONFIG_DIR}/Packages/VRTSvmsa.response \
-d ${VXPRODUCT} \
-R ${BASEDIR} VRTSvmsa
#
echo "Installing VRTSvmdoc..."
pkgadd -a ${SI_CONFIG_DIR}/Packages/noask \
-r ${SI_CONFIG_DIR}/Packages/VRTSvmdoc.response \
-d ${VXPRODUCT} \
-R ${BASEDIR} VRTSvmdoc
#
echo "Installing VRTSvmman..."
pkgadd -a ${SI_CONFIG_DIR}/Packages/noask \
-d ${VXPRODUCT} \
-R ${BASEDIR} VRTSvmman
#
echo "Installing VRTSvmdev..."
pkgadd -a ${SI_CONFIG_DIR}/Packages/noask \
-d ${VXPRODUCT} \
-R ${BASEDIR} VRTSvmdev
```

Note – For simplicity, we don't use a driver here. Normally, setting the environment variables (such as $BASEDIR) would be done in the driver.

The finish script does the actual installation of the unbundled product packages. The finish script name is specified in the rules file, from which it is automatically executed after the installation of the Solaris OE. The environment variable SI_CONFIG_DIR, automatically set by the JumpStart server, contains the path to the JumpStart directory specified in Step 3 by the -p option of add_install_client.

9. Create the `rules` file (or edit the existing `rules` file). Then verify the profile and `rules` file by executing the `check` script, generating `rules.ok`.

```
server01# cd /jumpstart
server01# cat rules
#
# The following rule matches any system:
#
any -    - \
Profiles/S8-server.profile \
Finish/install-S8-vxvm304.fin

server01# ./check
Validating rules...
Validating profile Profiles/S8-server.profile...
The custom JumpStart configuration is ok.
```

10. **Begin the installation.**

   `client03` is at the OpenBoot Prom (OBP) prompt, initiate the installation:

```
ok boot net - install
Resetting ...


Sun Ultra 1 UPA/SBus (UltraSPARC 167MHz), No Keyboard
OpenBoot 3.25, 128 MB memory installed, Serial #8191952.
Ethernet address 8:0:20:7c:ff:d0, Host ID: 807cffd0.


Rebooting with command: boot net - install
Boot device: /sbus/SUNW,hme@e,8c00000  File and args: - install
23e00
NOTICE: 64-bit OS installed, but the 32-bit OS is the default
   for the processor(s) on this system.
   See boot(1M) for more information.

Booting the 32-bit OS ...

SunOS Release 5.8 Version Generic_108528-07 32-bit
Copyright 1983-2001 Sun Microsystems, Inc.  All rights reserved.
whoami: no domain name
Configuring /dev and /devices
Using RPC Bootparams for network configuration information.
Configured interface hme0
Using sysid configuration file
10.1.1.5:/jumpstart/Sysidcfg/Solaris_8/sysidcfg
The system is coming up.  Please wait.
Starting remote procedure call (RPC) services: sysidns done.
Starting Solaris installation program...
Searching for JumpStart directory...
Using rules.ok from server01:/jumpstart.
Checking rules.ok file...
Using profile: Profiles/S8-server.profile
Using finish script: Finish/install-S8-vxvm304.fin
Executing JumpStart preinstall phase...
Searching for SolStart directory...
Checking rules.ok file...
Using begin script: install_begin
Using finish script: patch_finish
Executing SolStart preinstall phase...
Executing begin script "install_begin"...
Begin script install_begin execution completed.
```

After completion of the installation, verify it.

The installation is complete, `client03` has Solaris 8 OE, and VxVM 3.0.4 is installed.

```
client03# uname -a
SunOS client03 5.8 Generic_108528-07 sun4u sparc SUNW,Ultra-1
client03# cat /etc/release
                 Solaris 8 4/01 s28s_u4wos_08 SPARC
    Copyright 2001 Sun Microsystems, Inc.  All Rights Reserved.
                      Assembled 01 March 2001
client03# pkginfo | grep VRTS
system      VRTSvmdev   VERITAS Volume Manager, Header and Library Files
system      VRTSvmdoc   VERITAS Volume Manager (user documentation)
system      VRTSvmman   VERITAS Volume Manager, Manual Pages
system      VRTSvmsa    VERITAS Volume Manager Storage Administrator
system      VRTSvxvm    VERITAS Volume Manager, Binaries
client03# ls -al /etc/vx/reconfig.d/state.d
total 4
drwxr-xr-x   2 root      sys           512 Nov  2 16:26 .
drwxr-xr-x   5 root      sys           512 Nov  2 16:26 ..
-rw-r--r--   1 root      other           0 Nov  2 16:26 install-db
```

It is important to note that VxVM is not configured and that the `rootdg` disk group does not exist. Automatic encapsulation of the boot disk (and automating the initial configuration of VxVm software) is covered in the next section.

Automatic Interactive Configuration

This section presents techniques and procedures for automating the interactive configuration of software applications. It provides a detailed example of automating the initial configuration of the VXVM software and automatically encapsulating the root disk.

Since encapsulation is a complicated process, we'll first take a bird's-eye view of encapsulation. This section addresses only basic configuration and encapsulation of the root disk and is not meant to examine advanced techniques for installation of the Solaris OE and JumpStart server configuration. The techniques and procedures presented here are a starting point for your storage configuration and not a reference configuration for VxVM-controlled boot disks.

Note – This chapter uses the terms *boot disk* and *root disk* interchangeably to refer to the physical disk on which the Solaris OE is installed and in use as the default boot device.

Encapsulation—Brief Overview

Encapsulation is the method by which the VxVM software takes over management of a disk which has data that needs to be preserved. The most common use of encapsulation is to put the Solaris OE boot disk under VxVM software control. Placing the boot disk under VxVM software control is required to mirror the boot disk and to provide a higher level of reliability, availability, and serviceability (RAS) of the system.

All disks under VxVM software control (whether encapsulated or initialized) are divided into two regions:

1. Public region — Contains VxVM volumes, subdisks, and other logical devices.

2. Private region — Used by volume manager for internal storage of its configuration information.

When encapsulating a disk, the VxVM software requires a small amount of space (typically a cylinder) for its private region. This requirement poses a challenge in that this space may not have been planned for at the time the operating environment was installed. To work around this issue, when encapsulating the boot disk the VxVM software may steal several cylinders from the swap partition to be used as its private region. The VxVM software must then mask off the stolen area (to prevent it from being used as swap space) by creating a rootdiskPriv subdisk. You usually encapsulate the boot disk by running vxinstall or vxdiskadm and responding to the prompts.

Encapsulation—Looking Under the Hood

Because encapsulation is extremely interactive and difficult to script, the usual methods of encapsulation are not practicable for execution from a JumpStart finish script. To provide a hands-free method of invoking encapsulation, we use two techniques: hand-crafting VxVM control files directly and building the control files with /usr/lib/vxvm/bin/vxencap (the VxVM encapsulation preparation script).

The actual work of encapsulation is performed by /etc/init.d/vxvm-reconfig at system boot. vxvm-reconfig is driven by the contents or presence of several control files in the /etc/vx/reconfig.d directory.

Licensing

It is important to remember that the VxVM software requires a license. That license can be in the form of hardware such as a Sun StorEdge A5200 array or a software license key. Regardless of which licensing method is in use at your site, the VxVM software must be licensed before you attempt to encapsulate your boot disk.

If the software license method is in use at your site, the scripts and procedures presented here should be modified to license the VxVM product before any VxVM commands are executed or configuration is done. To create a software license, either modify the finish script to run `vxserial` or manually create the license key in the `/etc/vx/elm` directory.

vxvm-reconfig

All of the actual work of encapsulation, such as creating the private region and creating any needed subdisks, is done by `vxvm-reconfig`. Basically, `vxvm-reconfig` checks for the presence of several flag files and control files in `/etc/vx/reconfig.d`. Based on the presence and contents of these files `vxvm-reconfig` brings the disks under VxVM software control and makes other VxVM software configuration changes. An in-depth examination of `vxvm-reconfig` is outside the scope of this book. However, a careful reading of the script provides insight into the details of VxVM software startup.

vxencap-Created Control Files

The `vxencap` script creates the commands and does the encapsulated disk layout. By simply executing `vxencap` and specifying the desired disk media name (`rootdisk`), you set up the boot disk for encapsulation:

```
server01# /usr/lib/vxvm/bin/vxencap rootdisk=c0t0d0
```

`vxencap` is the preferred method for scripting encapsulation; it is a standard VxVM utility complete with a man page. However, `vxencap` does not function as expected from a JumpStart server finish script. The reason is that `vxencap` uses `vxparms` to query the environment and kernel. `vxparms` functions correctly from the finish script, but it returns information relative to the currently booted installation miniroot environment. The miniroot environment is different in several key areas, such as device major/minor numbers and device drivers. For example, the VxVM device drivers are not loaded in the JumpStart miniroot.

You can resolve this problem by enhancing the miniroot with the VxVM drivers, as detailed in Chapter 9, "Customizing JumpStart Framework for Installation and Recovery." However, working around the device numbering issues becomes problematic and inefficient in terms of time. The easiest method to maintain is having the JumpStart finish script add a startup script to the client system, such as /etc/rc3.d/S99encap-root, to be executed whenever the client system enters run-level three. S99encap-root tests for the presence of a flag file. If this flag file exists, then the S99encap-root script executes vxencap and initiates a reboot. At that reboot, vxvm-reconfig completes the actual work of encapsulating the boot disk.

When vxinstall is used to encapsulate the boot disk and configure VxVM, vxinstall gathers information on disks and disk controllers currently attached to the system and decides specifically what disks should be encapsulated and what disks need to be initialized. Our boot disk is c0t0d0, but there is one other disk on the c0 controller, c0t1d0. Therefore, we must manually create the files instructing VxVM to ignore c0t1d0.

We tell vxvm-reconfig to ignore disks by listing the disks to be ignored in a file named for the controller, and we then list, in the /etc/vx/reconfig.d/cntrls file, the controllers containing disks to be ignored. For example, the following two commands create and populate the files necessary to cause c0t1d0 to be ignored:

```
server01# echo c0t1d0 >/etc/vx/reconfig.d/c0
server01# echo c0 >/etc/vx/reconfig.d/cntrls
```

Finally, we signal vxvm-reconfig to reconfigure on the next reboot:

```
server01# touch /etc/vx/reconfig.d/state.d/reconfig
```

Finish Script for Automated Encapsulation After Installation

The profile, `sysidcfg` file, and server configuration are identical to those used in the previous installation example. Below is the JumpStart finish script used to install VxVM 3.0.4 and to automatically invoke encapsulation by creating the `S99encap-root` script and associated flag file.

```
#!/bin/sh

BASEDIR=/a
VXPRODUCT=${SI_CONFIG_DIR}/Packages/vxvm_3.0.4/pkgs
OK=0
NOTOK=1
#
echo "Installing VRTSvxvm..."
pkgadd -a ${SI_CONFIG_DIR}/Finish/noask \
-r ${SI_CONFIG_DIR}/Finish/S8-VRTSvxvm.response \
-d ${VXPRODUCT} \
-R ${BASEDIR} VRTSvxvm
#
echo "Installing VRTSvmsa..."
pkgadd -a ${SI_CONFIG_DIR}/Finish/noask \
-r ${SI_CONFIG_DIR}/Finish/VRTSvmsa.response \
-d ${VXPRODUCT} \
-R ${BASEDIR} VRTSvmsa
#
echo "Installing VRTSvmdoc..."
pkgadd -a ${SI_CONFIG_DIR}/Finish/noask \
-r ${SI_CONFIG_DIR}/Finish/VRTSvmdoc.response \
-d ${VXPRODUCT} \
-R ${BASEDIR} VRTSvmdoc
#
echo "Installing VRTSvmman..."
pkgadd -a ${SI_CONFIG_DIR}/Finish/noask \
-d ${VXPRODUCT} \
-R ${BASEDIR} VRTSvmman
#
echo "Installing VRTSvmdev..."
pkgadd -a ${SI_CONFIG_DIR}/Finish/noask \
-d ${VXPRODUCT} \
-R ${BASEDIR} VRTSvmdev
echo "Preparing for encapsulation of c0t0d0 ..."
```
(continued on next page)

```
(continued from previous page)
#
# Create any disk exclusion and inclusion files
#
cat > ${BASEDIR}/etc/rc3.d/S99encap-root <<EOENCAP-ROOT
#!/bin/sh

if [ ! -f /.S99encap-root-flag ]; then
        exit 0
fi

if [ ! -f /etc/vx/reconfig.d/state.d/install-db ]; then
        gettext "ERROR: S99encap-root: VxVM appears to be \
            already configured.\n"
        gettext "TO FIX: this setup program will not attempt\
            to reinitialize the system.\n"
        exit 1
fi
#
# If needed, setup of the software license would go here
#
# Verify the disk we are operating on is c0t0d0s0.
gettext "Verifying root device ... "
A="\'df -k / | awk '/^\/dev\// {print \$1}'\'"
if [ "\$A" != "/dev/dsk/c0t0d0s0" ]; then
        echo
        gettext "ERROR: S99encap-root: current boot device \
            must be /dev/dsk/c0t0d0s0.\n"
        gettext "TO FIX: ensure system is not yet configured \
            with VxVM.\n"
        exit 1
fi
gettext "ok.\n"

# Set up root disk for encapsulation, the actual encapsulation
# occurs at the next reboot.
/usr/lib/vxvm/bin/vxencap rootdisk=c0t0d0
echo c0t0d0 >/etc/vx/reconfig.d/disks-cap-part
echo c0t1d0 >/etc/vx/reconfig.d/c0
echo c0 >/etc/vx/reconfig.d/cntrls
touch /etc/vx/reconfig.d/state.d/init-cap-part
touch /etc/vx/reconfig.d/state.d/reconfig
```
(continued on next page)

```
(continued from previous page)
#
rm -f /.S99encap-root-flag
/sbin/init 6
EOENCAP-ROOT
chmod 755 ${BASEDIR}/etc/rc3.d/S99encap-root
touch ${BASEDIR}/.S99encap-root-flag
exit ${OK}
```

In this example, the boot disk has been encapsulated but not mirrored. Mirroring can be accomplished by addition of the appropriate commands to the script. Since detailed VxVM configuration is outside the scope of this book, it has been omitted.

Note – For simplicity, we don't use a driver here. Normally, setting the environment variables (such as $BASEDIR) would be done in the driver.

This method adds one reboot to the installation process: boot off the JumpStart server to install the Solaris OE, reboot off the newly installed disk, then reboot again after the vxencap completes. However, this is certainly an equitable trade-off for having an automated, documented, and easily maintainable method of installation and encapsulation.

Verifying Encapsulation

After doing a `boot net - install` with the preceding finish script specified, verify that the boot disk has indeed been encapsulated:

```
client03# uname -a
SunOS client03 5.8 Generic_108528-07 sun4u sparc SUNW,Ultra-1
client03# cat /etc/release
                      Solaris 8 4/01 s28s_u4wos_08 SPARC
            Copyright 2001 Sun Microsystems, Inc.  All Rights Reserved.
                         Assembled 01 March 2001
client03# pkginfo |grep VRTS
system      VRTSvmdev       VERITAS Volume Manager, Header and Library Files
system      VRTSvmdoc        VERITAS Volume Manager (user documentation)
system      VRTSvmman       VERITAS Volume Manager, Manual Pages
system      VRTSvmsa        VERITAS Volume Manager Storage Administrator
system      VRTSvxvm        VERITAS Volume Manager, Binaries
client03# ls -la /etc/vx/reconfig.d/state.d
total 4
drwxr-xr-x   2 root      sys            512 Nov  7 07:57 .
drwxr-xr-x   6 root      sys            512 Nov  7 07:55 ..
-rw-r--r--   1 root      root             0 Nov  7 07:55 root-done
client03# df -k
Filesystem             kbytes     used    avail capacity  Mounted on
/dev/vx/dsk/rootvol   1502255   786108   656057     55%   /
/proc                       0        0        0      0%   /proc
fd                          0        0        0      0%   /dev/fd
mnttab                      0        0        0      0%   /etc/mnttab
swap                   591200        0   591200      0%   /var/run
swap                   591208        8   591200      1%   /tmp
client03# vxprint -ht
Disk group: rootdg

DG NAME          NCONFIG       NLOG     MINORS   GROUP-ID
DM NAME          DEVICE        TYPE     PRIVLEN  PUBLEN   STATE
V  NAME          USETYPE       KSTATE   STATE    LENGTH   READPOL    PREFPLEX
PL NAME          VOLUME        KSTATE   STATE    LENGTH   LAYOUT     NCOL/WID  MODE
SD NAME          PLEX          DISK     DISKOFFS LENGTH   [COL/]OFF  DEVICE    MODE
SV NAME          PLEX          VOLNAME  NVOLLAYR LENGTH   [COL/]OFF  AM/NM     MODE

dg rootdg        default       default  0        973612541.1025.client03

dm rootdisk      c0t0d0s2      sliced   1519     4152640  -

v  rootvol       root          ENABLED  ACTIVE   3100800  ROUND      -
pl rootvol-01    rootvol       ENABLED  ACTIVE   3100800  CONCAT     -         RW
sd rootdisk-02   rootvol-01    rootdisk 1050319  3100800  0          c0t0d0    ENA

v  swapvol       swap          ENABLED  ACTIVE   1048800  ROUND      -
pl swapvol-01    swapvol       ENABLED  ACTIVE   1048800  CONCAT     -         RW
sd rootdisk-01   swapvol-01    rootdisk 1519     1048800  0          c0t0d0    ENA
```

Hand-Crafting Control Files

By hand-crafting the control files in `/etc/vx/reconfig.d` from the JumpStart server's finish script, you enable encapsulation to occur on the next reboot after the Solaris OE installation completes. This technique is presented only to provide an understanding of the encapsulation procedure. For reasons that shall soon become painfully apparent, this technique is not recommended.

The primary purpose of `vxencap` is to map out the specified disk for encapsulation. This mapping process involves specifying the subdisk layout information for the soon-to-be encapsulated disk and saving a copy of the disk's current volume table of contents (VTOC). This saved VTOC is required if the disk is ever to be unencapsulated and to revert to the underlying partitions. Additionally, you need to specify the disk media name that VxVM should use for the device. For every device to be encapsulated (controlled by the disk names listed in `/etc/vx/reconfig.d/disks-cap-part`), these items are stored in three files in a subdirectory named for the device, under the `/etc/vx/reconfig.d/disk.d` directory. For example, when encapsulating `/dev/dsk/c0t0d0`, the encapsulation control files you need to create are the following:

File Name	Contents
`/etc/vx/reconfig.d/disks-cap-part`	The disk(s) device names to be encapsulated
`/etc/vx/reconfig.d/disk.d/c0t0d0`	Directory
`/etc/vx/reconfig.d/disk.d/c0t0d0/dmname`	The media name for this disk
`/etc/vx/reconfig.d/disk.d/c0t0d0/newpart`	Subdisk layout
`/etc/vx/reconfig.d/disk.d/c0t0d0/vtoc`	VTOC

The contents of both the `newpart` and `vtoc` files depend on the underlying disk geometry. This implies that a unique file needs to be hand-crafted for each disk geometry to be encapsulated. You can use the VxVM utility `vxprtvtoc` to generate the `vtoc` file. The subdisk layout information and offsets, however, still need to be manually calculated and created for each disk.

Obviously, this procedure is a manual, labor-intensive process that is extremely susceptible to human error. Additionally, this procedure requires the system administrator to be intimately aware of the disk geometry of every disk to be encapsulated. Because the procedure has so many opportunities for error and very few checkpoints for verification, this technique cannot be recommended.

Automated Encapsulation from the Finish Script

The following code listing is the JumpStart server finish script from the previous section, augmented to automatically encapsulate the root disk (c0t0d0) after installation of the Solaris 8 OE and the VxVM 3.0.4 software. For this example, licensing is taken care of by the Sun StorEdge A5200 attached to client03.

As with any installation procedure or script, this script should be thoroughly tested and understood before being used. Initialization of disks by VxVM repartitions the disks, irrevocably erasing all preexisting data on the disks.

The finish script used for this example is:

```
#!/bin/sh

BASEDIR=/a
VXPRODUCT=${SI_CONFIG_DIR}/Packages/vxvm_3.0.4/pkgs
RECON=${BASEDIR}/etc/vx/reconfig.d
DISKD=${RECON}/disk.d
STATED=${RECON}/state.d
ROOTDEV=c0t0d0
OK=0
NOTOK=1
```

```
echo "Installing VRTSvxvm..."
pkgadd -a ${SI_CONFIG_DIR}/Finish/noask \
-r ${SI_CONFIG_DIR}/Finish/S8-VRTSvxvm.response \
-d ${VXPRODUCT} \
-R ${BASEDIR} VRTSvxvm
#
echo "Installing VRTSvmsa..."
pkgadd -a ${SI_CONFIG_DIR}/Finish/noask \
-r ${SI_CONFIG_DIR}/Finish/VRTSvmsa.response \
-d ${VXPRODUCT} \
-R ${BASEDIR} VRTSvmsa
#
echo "Installing VRTSvmdoc..."
pkgadd -a ${SI_CONFIG_DIR}/Finish/noask \
-r ${SI_CONFIG_DIR}/Finish/VRTSvmdoc.response \
-d ${VXPRODUCT} \
-R ${BASEDIR} VRTSvmdoc
#
echo "Installing VRTSvmman..."
pkgadd -a ${SI_CONFIG_DIR}/Finish/noask \
-d ${VXPRODUCT} \
-R ${BASEDIR} VRTSvmman
#
echo "Installing VRTSvmdev..."
pkgadd -a ${SI_CONFIG_DIR}/Finish/noask \
-d ${VXPRODUCT} \
-R ${BASEDIR} VRTSvmdev
echo "Preparing for encapsulation of c0t0d0 ..."
#
# If needed, setup software license would go here
#
# Create any disk exclusion and inclusion files
#
echo ${ROOTDEV} > ${RECON}/disks-cap-part
echo c0t1d0 > ${RECON}/c0
echo c0 > ${RECON}/cntrls
#
touch ${STATED}/init-cap-part
touch ${STATED}/reconfig
#
mkdir -p ${DISKD}/${ROOTDEV}
cat > ${DISKD}/${ROOTDEV}/newpart <<EOPART
```
(continued on next page)

```
(continued from previous page)
# volume manager partitioning for drive c0t0d0
 0 0x2 0x200  1050320  3100800
 1 0x3 0x201     1520  1048800
 2 0x5 0x200        0  4154160
 3 0xe 0x201        0  4154160
 4 0xf 0x201  4152640     1520
 5 0x0 0x000        0        0
 6 0x0 0x000        0        0
 7 0x0 0x000        0        0
#vxmake vol rootvol plex=rootvol-%%00 usetype=root logtype=none
#vxmake plex rootvol-%%00 sd=rootdisk-%%00
#vxmake sd rootdisk-%%00 disk=rootdisk offset=1050319 len=3100800
#vxvol start rootvol
#rename c0t0d0s0 rootvol
#vxmake vol swapvol plex=swapvol-%%01 usetype=swap
#vxmake plex swapvol-%%01 sd=rootdisk-%%01
#vxmake sd rootdisk-%%01 disk=rootdisk offset=1519 len=1048800
#vxvol start swapvol
#rename c0t0d0s1 swapvol
EOPART
chroot ${BASEDIR} /usr/lib/vxvm/bin/vxprtvtoc \
  -f /etc/vx/reconfig.d/disk.d/c0t0d0/vtoc /dev/dsk/c0t0d0
echo rootdisk > ${DISKD}/${ROOTDEV}/dmname
exit ${OK}
```

Note – For simplicity, we don't use a driver here. Normally, setting the environment variables (such as $BASEDIR) would be done in the driver.

Note that the newpart file created with the inline input redirection (or *here is file*) to the cat command contains several commented commands. These commands are commented out in the newpart file and are referenced later by the VxVM software when the VxVM plexes and subdisks are created.

Summary

In this chapter we examined the following issues:

- Procedures to fully automate patch installations
- Techniques to automate the interactive installation of software packages

Additionally, we looked at the mechanism of VxVM encapsulation of the boot disk and advanced JumpStart technology configuration techniques.

The techniques and procedures presented in this chapter are a starting point for adaptation of your storage configuration.

## CHAPTER 5

Automating Installations

This chapter describes how JumpStart installations can be automated through the use of repositories such as DHCP, NIS, NIS+, files, and diskettes. To illustrate the configuration processes of these various JumpStart techniques, this chapter presents a lab environment in which the various alternatives are implemented and described.

The first section of this chapter describes the way in which the lab environment is put together and the various servers installed. The second part of this chapter details each of the JumpStart technology automation techniques individually. Five distinct environments are presented to demonstrate recommended configurations.

This chapter describes the following topics:

- Test environment construction
- Hands-free installations

Test Environment Construction

A lab environment was constructed to illustrate the required JumpStart functionality in this chapter and Chapter 6, "JumpStart Internals," and to make it easier to describe and document the features of the JumpStart servers. The environments described in this chapter are intended to be used as a starting point for use in your datacenter. These environments were designed to provide a reference configuration as well as recommendations for developing a JumpStart solution specific to the needs of your environment.

Chapter 2, "JumpStart Overview," presented a less complex environment with the goal of simplifying the initial configuration and deployment of a JumpStart environment. This chapter delves much deeper into the component parts of JumpStart technology and correspondingly presents a more complicated topology.

Server Installation

This section provides step-by-step instructions on how to install and configure a JumpStart server and client running the Solaris 8 OE. Each step necessary in the configuration of the systems illustrates the commands and the associated output. Explanations of the JumpStart configuration files and options are also provided.

Based on the protocol used, whether it's RARP, DHCP, or several other options, the actual configuration of the systems varies. The base network layout and configuration is presented in this section. Specific requirements for a particular situation are described in each particular section.

The example presented in this chapter consists of the following systems:

- boot01
- config01
- install01
- nisplus01
- nis01
- dhcp01
- client01

The network diagram in FIGURE 5-1 illustrates the network topology used in the lab network.

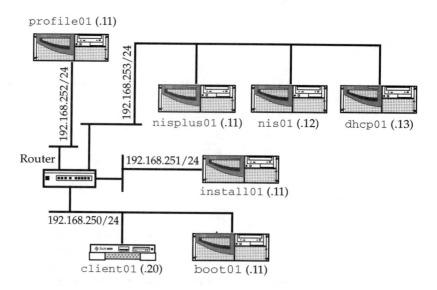

FIGURE 5-1 Network Diagram

Not all of these servers are used at the same time. For instance, only one name system is used simultaneously. The following table illustrates which servers are on (represented by the X) and which are off.

Repositories	boot01	nisplus01	nis01	dhcp01
NIS+	X	X		
NIS	X		X	
DHCP				X
Files	X			
Diskette				

The boot01 system functions as the JumpStart boot server for client01. The boot01 system provides the necessary services for the first- and second-level boot process during RARP-based installations. This system is not used during DHCP-based installations. In addition, boot01 provides the necessary information to the JumpStart client on how the JumpStart installation should use config01 and install01.

The config01 system provides the sysidcfg file. The configuration of this file varies, depending on the configuration of the rest of the environment. As mentioned earlier, this file is required to successfully automate a Solaris 8 OE JumpStart installation. The fully qualified path to the sysidcfg file is specified in the add_install_client command run on the JumpStart boot server. The config01 system shares this file with client01 over NFS.

The install01 system provides all the other information required for a successful JumpStart installation. This includes begin scripts, Solaris OE packages, finish scripts, and any other scripts used during the installation. This is the JumpStart server that makes the most use of the recommended JumpStart directories detailed in "Server Directory Architecture" on page 9 of Chapter 2.

The nis01 system provides NIS name service information to the client01 system when NIS is used as the repository. During installations when other repositories are used, this system is off.

The nisplus01 system provides NIS+ name service information to the client01 system when NIS+ is used as the repository. During installations when other repositories are used, this system is off.

A few steps are common to all types of JumpStart servers. The first step in building a JumpStart server is to install the appropriate Solaris OE. Once the Solaris OE is installed, the latest patch cluster available from SunSolve should be applied to the Solaris OE image. It is assumed, for this example, that all required network configuration, account management, and any other modifications required to make the system functional have also been performed.

Once these tasks have been applied, define a JumpStart partition with adequate space on the JumpStart server boot01, install01, and config01. The JumpStart configuration server requires the least amount of space, and the JumpStart install server requires the largest amount of space.

Only those installation steps common to all the servers were described in this section. The remaining steps required to complete each server's configuration are detailed in the following sections.

Installing the Boot Server

Any required Solaris images are copied into the /jumpstart/OS directory. The installation convention used is Solaris_<version #>_<4 digit year>-<2 digit month>. Since the installation process used in this chapter is based on Solaris 8 OE 4/01, the directory is named Solaris_8_2001-04. By creating different directories to store separate updates and releases of the Solaris OE, you can maintain fine-grained control for testing and deployment.

You begin the installation by running the setup_install_server command from the Solaris 8 OE CD. Although the creation of a JumpStart install server changed with the Solaris 8 OE, the installation of a JumpStart boot server did *not*.

To create a Solaris 8 OE JumpStart server, insert the first Solaris 8 OE Software CD into the CD-ROM drive and enter the following commands:

```
boot01# pwd
/cdrom/sol_8_401_sparc/s0/Solaris_8/Tools
boot01# ./setup_install_server -b /jumpstart/OS/Solaris_8_2001-04
```

The -b flag of setup_install_server sets up the server as a boot server only. For additional details, see the setup_install_server man page. The preceding command produces the following output:

```
Verifying target directory...
Calculating the required disk space for the Solaris_8 product
Copying the CD image to disk...
Install Server setup complete
```

This completes the installation of the required Solaris OE source into the /jumpstart directory hierarchy. After the Solaris 8 OE software is installed on the JumpStart server, the /jumpstart directory must be made available to the JumpStart clients through the NFS system. Therefore, add the following line to the /etc/dfs/dfstab file:

```
share -F nfs -o ro,anon=0 -d "Jumpstart Directory" /jumpstart
```

Enter this command to execute the share command listed above:

```
boot01# shareall
```

Installing the Configuration Server

The JumpStart configuration server is the simplest server to set up because it uses only one of the directories in the recommended JumpStart directory structure. The profile information is kept in the /jumpstart/Sysidcfg directory. Because these examples use Solaris 8 OE, this directory is /jumpstart/Sysidcfg/Solaris_8.

Within the /jumpstart/Sysidcfg directory, create separate subdirectories for each of the Solaris OE versions supported by the JumpStart infrastructure. Separate directories are required because new keywords added to several Solaris OE releases are not recognized by other Solaris OE installations. If an unknown keyword is encountered during a JumpStart installation, the installation reverts to interactive mode.

Installing the Install Server

As discussed in "Installing the Boot Server" on page 90, create a directory in the /jumpstart/OS directory for each Solaris OE release. The installation convention used is Solaris_<version #>_<4 digit year>-<2 digit month>. Since the installation process used in this chapter is based on the Solaris 8 OE 4/01, the directory is named Solaris_8_2001-04. By creating different directories to store separate updates and releases of the Solaris OE, you maintain fine-grained control for testing and deployment.

The installation uses the same command as the setup of the JumpStart boot server, but with a different set of arguments. You begin the installation by running the setup_install_server command from the Solaris OE CD. The following procedure uses the Solaris 8 OE—however, this makes the JumpStart server installation process slightly different from installation processes that use earlier versions of the Solaris OE.

To create a Solaris 8 OE JumpStart server, insert the first Solaris 8 Software CD (labeled 1 of 2) into the CD-ROM drive and enter the following commands:

```
install01# pwd
/cdrom/sol_8_401_sparc/s0/Solaris_8/Tools
install01# ./setup_install_server /jumpstart/OS/Solaris_8_2001-04
```

This command produces the following output:

```
Verifying target directory...
Calculating the required disk space for the Solaris_8 product
Copying the CD image to disk...
Install Server setup complete
```

The first CD of the Solaris 8 OE is now installed. Insert the second CD (labeled 2 of 2) into the CD-ROM drive and enter the following commands:

```
install01# pwd
/cdrom/sol_8_401_sparc_2/Solaris_8/Tools
install01# ./add_to_install_server /jumpstart/OS/Solaris_8_2001-04
```

This command produces the following output:

```
The following Products will be copied to
/jumpstart/OS/Solairs_8_2001-04/Solaris_8/Product:

Solaris_2_of_2

If only a subset of products is needed enter Control-C
and invoke ./add_to_install_server with the -s option.

Checking required disk space...

Copying the Early Access products...
41990 blocks

Processing completed successfully.
```

After the Solaris 8 OE software is installed on the installation server, the /jumpstart directory must be made available to the JumpStart clients through the NFS system. Therefore, add the following line to the /etc/dfs/dfstab file:

```
share -F nfs -o ro,anon=0 -d "Jumpstart Directory" /jumpstart
```

Enter this command to execute the share command:

```
install01# shareall
```

Client Configuration Information

For a JumpStart software installation to be successful, the JumpStart infrastructure must have access to the Ethernet address (MAC) and IP addresses of the JumpStart client(s). This information can be provided to the JumpStart server through a repository such as NIS+, NIS, or DHCP or through the /etc/hosts and /etc/ethers files.

The server managing the repository is responsible for providing the client MAC and IP addresses to the JumpStart infrastructure. Depending on the repository used, the system providing this information changes.

The repository must contain the following MAC address of the client:

```
8:0:20:a0:3d:68 client01
```

The following IP address must also be in the repository:

```
192.168.250.20 client01
```

Lab Rules Definition

The rules file used for the lab network specified only a profile. Neither a begin nor a finish script is specified. The following line is defined:

```
hostname client01 - Profiles/entire-distribution.profile -
```

Lab Profile Definition

Use the profile named `entire-distribution.profile` for the JumpStart lab environment.

```
install_type     initial_install

cluster          SUNWCall

partitioning     explicit
filesys          rootdisk.s1     512 swap
filesys          rootdisk.s0     free    /

system_type      standalone
```

Hands-Free Installations

One of the main benefits JumpStart confers is the capability to fully automate JumpStart client installations so that no human intervention is required. One mechanism you can use to provide the required information to a JumpStart client is the `sysidcfg` file; see additional details in Chapter 2, "JumpStart Overview."

This section details other mechanisms capable of providing this information to a JumpStart client. The mechanisms include NIS, NIS+, DHCP, files, and diskettes. Since the release of the Solaris 8 OE, it is no longer possible to provide all the required JumpStart information through a name service. The reason is that `security_policy` and `protocol_ipv6` were added to the Solaris 8 OE and JumpStart software requires information on whether these options should be enabled or disabled on the JumpStart client. Unfortunately, this information cannot be shared through a name service. So even when all the other information is provided through a name service, a `sysidcfg` file with `security_policy` and `protocol_ipv6` is still required.

For each repository, this section instructs you on how to configure the basics of the repository itself and advises you about additional information required by JumpStart.

NIS Repository

NIS was originally known as YP and has been included as YP with the Solaris OE since the early releases of SunOS™ software. In this section, a basic NIS server is configured for use as the JumpStart client name service. Only those options required for a hands-free JumpStart software installation are presented here.

Setting Up the NIS Server

The first step in setting up an NIS server is to install the Solaris 8 OE on an appropriate system. In the examples below, this system is called nis01. The following commands are required to turn it into an NIS server.

The domain used for this example is blueprints.sun.com. Substitute a domain name appropriate for your organization.

```
nis01# echo 'blueprints.sun.com' > /etc/defaultdomain
nis01# domainname blueprints.sun.com
```

Next, populate the files (managed by NIS) with the required information:

Create an /etc/ethers file, and add a line similar to the following:

```
8:0:20:a0:3d:68 client01
```

Add the following line (for the JumpStart client) to the `/etc/hosts` file:

```
192.168.250.20 client01
```

In addition, the hosts file must also have an entry for *timehost* similar to the following:

```
192.168.251.11 install01     timehost
```

Verify that the correct time zone is defined in the `/etc/timezone` with the following command:

```
nis01# echo 'US/Eastern blueprints.sun.com' > /etc/timezone
```

Create an `/etc/netmasks` file containing the following information for any networks in which there are JumpStart clients.

```
192.168.250.0    255.255.255.0
```

Next, initialize the NIS server by running the `ypinit` script as follows:

```
nis01# cd /var/yp
nis01# /usr/sbin/ypinit -m
In order for NIS to operate successfully, we have to construct a
list of the NIS servers.  Please continue to add the names for YP
servers in order of preference, one per line.  When you are done
with the list, type a <control D> or a return on a line by itself.
        next host to add: nis01
        next host to add:  ^D
The current list of yp servers looks like this:

nis01

Is this correct?  [y/n: y] y

Installing the YP database will require that you answer a few
questions. Questions will all be asked at the beginning of the
procedure.

Do you want this procedure to quit on non-fatal errors? [y/n: n] n
OK, please remember to go back and redo manually whatever fails.
If you don't, some part of the system (perhaps the yp itself) won't
work. The yp domain directory is /var/yp/blueprints.sun.com
There will be no further questions. The remainder of the procedure
should take 5 to 10 minutes.
Building /var/yp/blueprints.sun.com/ypservers...
Running /var/yp /Makefile...
updated passwd
[...]
make: Warning: Target 'all' not remade because of errors
Current working directory /var/yp
*** Error code 1
make: Fatal error: Command failed for target 'k'
Error running Makefile.

nis01 has been set up as a yp master server with errors.  Please
remember to figure out what went wrong, and fix it.

If there are running slave yp servers, run yppush now for any
databases which have been changed.  If there are no running slaves,
run ypinit on those hosts which are to be slave servers.
```

Don't worry about errors. They just indicate that some maps weren't populated. This is not important for the JumpStart software installation.

At this time, reboot the system. It reboots as an NIS server. Verify this with the following commands:

```
nis01# ypwhich
nis01
nis01# ypcat hosts
192.168.250.20 client01
127.0.0.1        localhost loghost
[...]
nis01# ypcat ethers
8:0:20:a0:3d:68 client01
```

Obviously, the JumpStart boot server, boot01, must also be an NIS client for the add_install_client command to work.

Configuring the boot01 NIS Client

To configure boot01 as an NIS client, perform the following steps.

First, set the domain name by using the following commands:

```
boot01# echo 'blueprints.sun.com' > /etc/defaultdomain
boot01# domainname blueprints.sun.com
```

Next, configure the name resolution to use NIS, instead of the default files. Modify this behavior with the following command:

```
boot01# cp /etc/nsswitch.nis /etc/nsswitch.conf
```

NIS can now be started. The recommended solution is to start NIS in the following manner:

```
boot01# ypinit -c
In order for NIS to operate successfully, we have to construct a
list of the NIS servers.  Please continue to add the names for YP
servers in order of preference, one per line.  When you are done
with the list, type a <control D>
or a return on a line by itself.
        next host to add: nis01
        next host to add:   ^D
The current list of yp servers looks like this:

nis01

Is this correct?  [y/n: y]  y
```

At this time, reboot the system. It reboots as an NIS client. Verify this with the following commands:

```
boot01# ypwhich
nis01
boot01# ypcat hosts
192.168.250.20 client01
127.0.0.1       localhost loghost
[...]
boot01# ypcat ethers
8:0:20:a0:3d:68 client01
```

At this point, the NIS server is functioning and the JumpStart client installation can begin. Add the client to boot01 with the add_install_client in the following manner:

```
boot01# ./add_install_client \
-s install01:/jumpstart/OS/Solaris_8_2001-04 \
-c install01:/jumpstart \
-n nis01:nis\(255.255.255.0\) \
-p config01:/jumpstart/Sysidcfg/Solaris_8 client01 sun4u
```

See the add_install_client(1M) man page for additional details.

The preceding commands produce the following output:

```
saving original /etc/dfs/dfstab in /etc/dfs/dfstab.orig
Adding "share -F nfs -o ro,anon=0 /jumpstart/OS/Solaris_8_2001-
04/Solaris_8/Tools/Boot" to /etc/dfs/dfstab
making /tftpboot
enabling tftp in /etc/inetd.conf
starting rarpd
bootparams: nis [NOTFOUND=return] files
changed bootparams entry in /etc/nsswitch.conf
starting bootparamd
starting nfsd's
starting nfs mountd
updating /etc/bootparams
copying inetboot to /tftpboot
```

Configuring `sysidcfg` for NIS

The rest of the JumpStart infrastructure servers in this example (that is, config01 and install01) have already been configured. The sysidcfg file on config01 must contain at least the following information:

```
system_locale=en_US
network_interface=hme0 {protocol_ipv6=no}
security_policy=NONE
terminal=vt100
root_password=jPxa1fICIVZI6
```

Installing the Client

After boot01 is restarted, verify that all the name services and other daemons are functioning properly by beginning the JumpStart installation on client01 with the following command:

```
ok boot net - install
```

The output of the JumpStart software installation looks like this:

```
ok boot net - install
Resetting ...

Sun Ultra 5/10 UPA/PCI (UltraSPARC-IIi 270MHz), No Keyboard
OpenBoot 3.11, 192 MB memory installed, Serial #10501480.
Ethernet address 8:0:20:a0:3d:68, Host ID: 80a03d68.

Rebooting with command: boot net - install
Boot device: /pci@1f,0/pci@1,1/network@1,1  File and args: -
install
SunOS Release 5.8 Version Generic_108528-07 64-bit
Copyright 1983-2001 Sun Microsystems, Inc.  All rights reserved.
Configuring /dev and /devices
Using RPC Bootparams for network configuration information.
Configured interface hme0
Using sysid configuration file
192.168.252.11:/jumpstart/Sysidcfg/Solaris_8/sysidcfg
The system is coming up.  Please wait.
Starting remote procedure call (RPC) services: sysidns done.
Starting Solaris installation program...
Searching for JumpStart directory...
Using rules.ok from 192.168.251.11:/jumpstart.
Checking rules.ok file...
Using profile: Profiles/entire-distribution.profile
Executing JumpStart preinstall phase...
Searching for SolStart directory...
Checking rules.ok file...
Using begin script: install_begin
Using finish script: patch_finish
Executing SolStart preinstall phase...
Executing begin script "install_begin"...
Begin script install_begin execution completed.
```

This installation didn't require any user intervention (interactive installation) during the process. The client, client01, successfully installed the Solaris 8 OE and rebooted as an NIS client. The only oddity is that the use of the root_password argument in sysidcfg prevents the system from prompting for a root password, but only when the JumpStart client is installed with the Solaris OE End User, Developer, or Entire clusters. When the minimal or Required cluster is being installed, the root_password entry in the sysidcfg is ignored and the system comes up without a root password after installation.

NIS+ Repository

NIS+ is an enhanced version of NIS. Most of the enhancements are in the area of security and hierarchical domains. This section walks you through the minimum required steps to build an NIS+ server that provides information to a JumpStart client. Only those parts applicable to the NIS+ environment are described in the following sections.

Setting Up the NIS+ Server

The first step in setting up an NIS+ server is to install the Solaris 8 OE on it. For this example, the NIS+ server, called nisplus01, has Solaris 8 OE 4/01 installed on it. Once Solaris 8 OE is installed, the following required commands turn nisplus01 into an NIS+ server.

The domain used for this example is blueprints.sun.com. Substitute a domain name appropriate for your organization.

```
nisplus01# domainname blueprints.sun.com.
nisplus01# echo 'blueprints.sun.com.' > /etc/defaultdomain
nisplus01# echo 'US/Eastern blueprints.sun.com.' > /etc/timezone
```

After you have specified this configuration information-initialize nisplus01 as an NIS+ server with this command:

```
nisplus01# /usr/lib/nis/nisserver -v -r -d blueprints.sun.com.
```

While the following output is being produced, several questions are asked that you must answer:

```
This script sets up this machine "nisplus01" as an NIS+
root master server for domain blueprints.sun.com..

Domain name             : blueprints.sun.com.
NIS+ group              : admin.blueprints.sun.com.
NIS (YP) compatibility  : OFF
Security level          : 2=DES

Is this information correct? (type 'y' to accept, 'n' to change) y

This script will set up your machine as a root master server for
domain blueprints.sun.com. without NIS compatibility at security
level 2.
Enter login password: xxxxxx

creating NIS+ administration group: admin.blueprints.sun.com. ...
adding principal nisplus01.blueprints.sun.com. to
admin.blueprints.sun.com. ...

updating the keys for directories ...

restarting NIS+ root master server at security level 2 ...
killing process rpc.nisd ...
restarting process rpc.nisd ...
starting NIS+ password daemon ...
starting NIS+ cache manager ...
modifying the /etc/init.d/rpc file ...
starting Name Service Cache Daemon nscd ...

This system is now configured as a root server for domain
blueprints.sun.com.
You can now populate the standard NIS+ tables by using the
nispopulate script or /usr/lib/nis/nisaddent command.
```

At this point, reboot `nisplus01`, verify the NIS+ server configuration by running the following NIS+ commands, and also verify that there are no errors.

```
nisplus01# /usr/bin/nisls
nisplus01# /usr/bin/niscat passwd.org_dir
```

To automate a JumpStart installation, populate only the `bootparams`, `ethers`, `hosts`, `netmasks`, and `timezone` files in the NIS+ maps on `nisplus01`. To populate these maps, copy the contents of these files to a temporary working directory `/var/tmp/nisfiles`. These are all small ASCII files. You must populate the following NIS+ maps in order for a hands-free (automated) NIS+ installation to function properly:

- `ethers`
- `hosts`
- `netmasks`
- `rpc`
- `services`
- `timezone`

To automate the JumpStart software installation of `client01`, populate the files as follows:

```
nisplus01# pwd
/var/tmp/nisfiles
nisplus01# more ethers
8:0:20:a0:3d:68 client01
nisplus01# more hosts
127.0.0.1 localhost
192.168.250.11 boot01
192.168.250.20 client01
192.168.251.11 install01
192.168.252.11 config01
192.168.253.11 nisplus01 timehost
nisplus01# more netmasks
192.168.250.0      255.255.255.0
nisplus01# more timezone
US/Eastern       blueprints.sun.com.
nisplus01# more services
[...]
nisplus01# more rpc
[...]
```

Note – The host name `timehost` must be assigned to a host in the NIS+ *hosts* map to preclude the JumpStart client from asking for time information during installation.

Verify that the NIS+ hosts table has an entry for the client. If it does not, add it to the appropriate file, then use `nispopulate` to add it to the NIS+ tables.

Once these files are populated, the NIS+ maps can be updated with the following command:

```
nisplus01# pwd
/var/tmp/nisfiles
nisplus01# /usr/lib/nis/nispopulate -v -F
This script sets up this machine "nisplus01" as an NIS+
root master server for domain blueprints.sun.com..

Domain name             : blueprints.sun.com.
NIS+ group              : admin.blueprints.sun.com.
NIS (YP) compatibility  : OFF
Security level          : 2=DES

Is this information correct? (type 'y' to accept, 'n' to change) y

This script will set up your machine as a root master server for
domain blueprints.sun.com. without NIS compatibility at security
level 2.

Use "nisclient -r" to restore your current network service
environment.

Do you want to continue? (type 'y' to continue, 'n' to exit this
script) y

setting up domain information "blueprints.sun.com." ...
[...]
```

If any errors are encountered, modify and reload the appropriate file with the command `nispopulate -v -F -u <file-name>`.

Once again, reboot `nisplus01`, verify the NIS+ server configuration by running the following NIS+ commands, and also verify that there are no errors.

```
nisplus01# /usr/bin/nisls
nisplus01# /usr/bin/niscat ethers.org_dir
8:0:20:a0:3d:68 client01
```

Run the `nisclient` script to add credentials for any NIS+ client systems. In the case of the `blueprints.sun.com` test network, the client system is `boot01` and the command has the following syntax.

```
nisplus01# /usr/lib/nis/nisclient -v -d blueprints.sun.com. \
-c boot01
```

Do not be concerned if `nisclient` tells you that the credentials already exist for your `client_machine`. The previous step is not required, but it makes the process clearer and ensures that the appropriate credentials have been created.

One additional table must be created within NIS+, one that provides the JumpStart client with the default language for installation. The following example sets English as the default language.

The first step to making the default language available over NIS+ is to create an NIS+ table called `locale`. Create this table with the following command on the NIS+ server, `nisplus01`.

```
nisplus01# /usr/bin/nistbladm -D access=og=rmcd,nw=r -c \ locale_tbl
name=SI,nogw= locale=,nogw= comment=,nogw= \
locale.org_dir.'nisdefaults -d'
```

Next, populate this new NIS+ table with the following command:

```
nisplus01# /usr/bin/nistbladm -a name=blueprints.sun.com. \
locale=C comment=English locale.org_dir.'nisdefaults -d'
```

Verify your previous actions with the following command to ensure that everything works properly.

```
nisplus01# /usr/bin/niscat locale.org_dir
blueprints.sun.com. C English
```

Configuring the `boot01` NIS+ Client

Setting up `boot01` as an NIS+ client involves the following steps.

The domain used for this example is `blueprints.sun.com`, set as follows:

```
boot01# domainname blueprints.sun.com.
boot01# echo 'blueprints.sun.com.' > /etc/defaultdomain
```

Next, run `nisclient` to initialize `boot01` as an NIS+ client:

```
boot01# /usr/lib/nis/nisclient -v -i -h nisplus01 \
-a 192.168.253.11 -d blueprints.sun.com.
initializing client machine...

Initializing client boot01 for domain "blueprints.sun.com.".
Once initialization is done, you will need to reboot your
machine.

Do you want to continue? (type 'y' to continue, 'n' to exit this
script) y

killing NIS and/or NIS+ processes...
killing process ypbind...
killing process nis_cachemgr...
killing process rpc.nispasswdd...
stopping nscd ...

setting up backup files...
setting up NIS+ server information...
setting up domain information "blueprints.sun.com."...

setting up the name service switch information...
killing process keyserv...


running nisinit command ...
nisinit -c -H 192.168.253.11 ...

credential exists for setting up security...
setting up security information for root...
At the prompt below, type the network password (also known
as the Secure-RPC password) that you obtained either
from your administrator or from running the nispopulate script.
Please enter the Secure-RPC password for root: xxxxxxxx
Please enter the login password for root: xxxxxxxx

Your network password has been changed to your login one.
Your network and login passwords are now the same.

killing process nis_cachemgr...

starting nscd ...
Client initialization completed!!
Please reboot your machine for changes to take effect.
```

After rebooting `boot01`, verify that the NIS+ maps have been initialized correctly. For example, use the following commands to verify the password map.

```
boot01# /usr/bin/nisls
boot01# /usr/bin/niscat passwd.org_dir
```

Installing the Client

At this point, add the JumpStart client to the boot server with the following `add_install_client` command.

```
boot01# add_install_client \
-s install01:/jumpstart/OS/Solaris_8_2001-04 \
-c install01:/jumpstart \
-n nisplus01:nisplus\(255.255.255.0\) \
-p config01:/jumpstart/Sysidcfg/Solaris_8 \
client01 sun4u
```

In this `add_install_client` command, use the `-n` option to specify both the name service type (for example, NIS+) and the netmask of the network on which the NIS+ server is located.

The `sysidcfg` file specified by the `-p` option contains only the two pieces of information that cannot be provided through the NIS+ maps. The `sysidcfg` file looks like this:

```
config01# pwd
/jumpstart/Sysidcfg/Solaris_8
config01# more sysidcfg
network_interface=hme0 {protocol_ipv6=no}
security_policy=NONE
root_password=jPxa1fICIVZI6
```

The following is the output generated during the JumpStart software installation of client01, using the configuration defined here:

```
ok boot net - install
Resetting ...

Sun Ultra 5/10 UPA/PCI (UltraSPARC-IIi 270MHz), No Keyboard
OpenBoot 3.11, 192 MB memory installed, Serial #10501480.
Ethernet address 8:0:20:a0:3d:68, Host ID: 80a03d68.

Rebooting with command: boot net - install
Boot device: /pci@1f,0/pci@1,1/network@1,1  File and args: -
install
SunOS Release 5.8 Version Generic_108528-07 64-bit
Copyright 1983-2001 Sun Microsystems, Inc.  All rights reserved.
Configuring /dev and /devices
Using RPC Bootparams for network configuration information.
Configured interface hme0
Using sysid configuration file
192.168.252.11:/jumpstart/Sysidcfg/Solaris_8/sysidcfg
The system is coming up.  Please wait.
Starting remote procedure call (RPC) services: sysidns done.
Starting Solaris installation program...
Searching for JumpStart directory...
Using rules.ok from 192.168.251.11:/jumpstart.
Checking rules.ok file...
Using profile: Profiles/entire-distribution.profile
Executing JumpStart preinstall phase...
Searching for SolStart directory...
Checking rules.ok file...
Using begin script: install_begin
Using finish script: patch_finish
Executing SolStart preinstall phase...
Executing begin script "install_begin"...
Begin script install_begin execution completed.
```

DHCP Repository

With the release of sun4u and OpenBoot PROM (OBP) release 3.x, it has become possible to provide a JumpStart client with its IP address by using DHCP instead of RARP. This provision affords a significant improvement in WAN usability because it is no longer necessary to have a boot server on each subnet.

To demonstrate the use of DHCP, we JumpStart the JumpStart client used in these examples, client01, without boot01 providing initial boot services from the local subnet as with the other JumpStart technology examples in this chapter. Instead, the add_install_client script is run on install01, which is on a different subnet from client01. In addition, the DHCP server, dhcp01, is also located on a separate subnet from client01.

Use OpenBoot PROM (OBP) version 3.25 or later to support DHCP Jumpstart installations. Patches are available on SunSolve to update the OBP.

For the test environment used in this chapter, we used dhcpconfig to configure the gateway system as a BOOTP/DHCP relay.

There are two parts to the configuration of the network to support DHCP JumpStarts:

- Configure install01 to provide the JumpStart information to client01.
- Configure the DHCP server to provide client01 with its IP address on boot.

Configuring install01

The /etc/hosts files on install01 includes an entry for client01 and looks like this:

```
install01# more hosts
127.0.0.1 localhost
192.168.250.11 boot01
192.168.250.20 client01
192.168.251.11 install01
192.168.252.11 config01
192.168.253.11 nisplus01 timehost
```

At this time, the JumpStart client installation begins. Add the client to install01 in the following manner:

```
install01# ./add_install_client -d \
-c install01:/jumpstart \
-p config01:/jumpstart/Sysidcfg/Solaris_8 \
client01 sun4u
```

The preceding commands produce the following output:

```
making /tftpboot
enabling tftp in /etc/inetd.conf
copying inetboot to /tftpboot
To enable client01 in the DHCP server,
add an entry to the server with the following data:

Install server       (SinstNM) : install01
Install server path  (SinstPTH): /jumpstart/OS/Solaris_8_2001-04
Root server name     (SrootNM) : install01
Root server path     (SrootPTH): /jumpstart/OS/Solaris_8_2001-
04/Solaris_8/Tools/Boot
Profile location     (SjumpsCF): install01:/jumpstart
sysidcfg location    (SsysidCF):
config01:/jumpstart/Sysidcfg/Solaris_8
```

Now it is necessary to configure the DHCP server and BOOTP relay, if necessary, so that they provide the correct information to the JumpStart client.

DHCP requests, in much the same fashion as RARP requests, are protocols that are not normally routed. DHCP requests are much easier than RARP requests to honor. When a DHCP server is not available on the local subnet, DHCP client requests can use a BOOTP relay to forward requests from the local subnet to a central DHCP server. The Solaris 8 OE includes the functionality to do this, as do many routers. For additional details refer to the dhcpmgr(1M) man page.

Configuring dhcp01

The configuration of the DHCP server is the most critical part of this configuration. DHCP server software is included with the Solaris 8 OE and can be updated either through the graphical user interface (GUI) or command-line interface (CLI). The following Solaris OE packages must be installed for the DHCP software to work properly.

```
dhcp01# pkginfo | grep -i dhcp
system        SUNWdhcm        DHCP Manager
system        SUNWdhcsr       BOOTP/DHCP Server Services, (Root)
system        SUNWdhcsu       BOOTP/DHCP Server Services, (Usr)
```

Note – These packages are not installed by default on Solaris OE systems except when the SUNWCall installation cluster is used.

The required startup and shutdown scripts in /etc/init.d are installed by these packages. The in.dhcpd daemon is started by default whenever the system is booted.

All configuration information for the DHCP server is maintained in the dhcptab macro file stored in /var/dhcp. The contents of this file can be modified either through the DHCP Manager GUI, /usr/sadm/admin/bin/dhcpmgr, or by direct editing of the macro definition file /var/dhcp/dhcptab.

For additional information about the DHCP Manager GUI, see the dhcpmgr(1M) man page. Additional information about the DHCP macro definition file, dhcptab, can be found in the dhcptab(4) man page.

For more about using the dhcpmgr GUI and for additional information on configuring the DHCP server, refer to Volume 3 of the *System Administration Guide* in the section titled "Configuring DHCP Service." Additional information on how to configure a DHCP server to support JumpStart client installations is available in the section titled "Supporting Solaris Network Install Clients with DHCP Service." These manuals are available at http://docs.sun.com.

In this example, the dhcptab macro definition file was edited directly. The dhcpmgr GUI was not used.

The `/var/dhcp/dhcptab` used on dhcp01 to automate the installation of client01, which is an Ultra™ 5 workstation, contains the following information.

```
Locale    m        :UTCoffst=-18000:
dhcp01        m :Include=Locale:Timeserv=192.168.253.13:LeaseTim=86400:LeaseNeg:
192.168.250.0    m
:Subnet=255.255.255.0:MTU=1500:Router=192.168.250.10:Broadcst=192.168.250.255:BootS
rvA=192.168.251.11:
SrootOpt        s Vendor=SUNW.Ultra-1 SUNW.Ultra-5_10,1,ASCII,1,0
SrootIP4        s Vendor=SUNW.Ultra-1 SUNW.Ultra-5_10,2,IP,1,1
SrootNM         s Vendor=SUNW.Ultra-1 SUNW.Ultra-5_10,3,ASCII,1,0
SrootPTH        s Vendor=SUNW.Ultra-1 SUNW.Ultra-5_10,4,ASCII,1,0
SswapIP4        s Vendor=SUNW.Ultra-1 SUNW.Ultra-5_10,5,IP,1,0
SswapPTH        s Vendor=SUNW.Ultra-1 SUNW.Ultra-5_10,6,ASCII,1,0
SbootFIL        s Vendor=SUNW.Ultra-1 SUNW.Ultra-5_10,7,ASCII,1,0
Stz             s Vendor=SUNW.Ultra-1 SUNW.Ultra-5_10,8,ASCII,1,0
SbootRS         s Vendor=SUNW.Ultra-1 SUNW.Ultra-5_10,9,NUMBER,2,1
SinstIP4        s Vendor=SUNW.Ultra-1 SUNW.Ultra-5_10,10,IP,1,1
SinstNM         s Vendor=SUNW.Ultra-1 SUNW.Ultra-5_10,11,ASCII,1,0
SinstPTH        s Vendor=SUNW.Ultra-1 SUNW.Ultra-5_10,12,ASCII,1,0
SsysidCF        s Vendor=SUNW.Ultra-1 SUNW.Ultra-5_10,13,ASCII,1,0
SjumpsCF        s Vendor=SUNW.Ultra-1 SUNW.Ultra-5_10,14,ASCII,1,0
Sterm           s Vendor=SUNW.Ultra-1 SUNW.Ultra-5_10,15,ASCII,1,0
Solaris       m
:SrootIP4=192.168.251.11:SrootNM="install01":SinstIP4=192.168.251.11:SinstNM="insta
l
101":Sterm="xterm":SjumpsCF="install01:/jumpstart":SsysidCF="192.168.252.11:/jumpst
art/Sysidcfg/Solaris_8":
sparc         m        :SrootPTH="/jumpstart/OS/Solaris_8_2001-
04/Solaris_8/Tools/Boot":SinstPTH="/jumpstart/OS/Solaris
_8_2001-04":
sun4u         m        :Include=Solaris:Include=sparc:
SUNW.Ultra-1    m        :SbootFIL="/platform/sun4u/kernel/unix":Include=sun4u:
SUNW.Ultra-5_10 m
:SbootFIL="/platform/sun4u/kernel/sparcv9/unix":Include=sun4u:
```

The creation of this configuration is a combination of the documentation in the *System Administration Guide*, the output of the add_install_client command, and some trial and error. The fundamental concepts are not well documented and the question was into which macro should the definitions of SsysidCF and SjumpCF be placed. After experimenting with the SUNW.Ultra-5_10, sparc, and several other macro definitions, we discovered that these fields *must* be included within the Solaris macro definition.

Appropriate definitions of the specific Sun hardware being installed must have its Vendor System Class (for example, SUNW.Ultra-5_10 and SUNW.Ultra-1) added to the dhcptab. The previous example included definitions for the Ultra 5, Ultra 10, and Ultra 1 systems. For additional details, refer to the *Solaris Administration Guide* sections listed previously in this section.

Resolving an Undocumented Issue

One undocumented issue was encountered during the development of this process. When the previous configuration was defined and implemented, the following error was encountered by the JumpStart client client01.

```
ok boot net:dhcp - install
Resetting ...
Sun Ultra 5/10 UPA/PCI (UltraSPARC-IIi 270MHz), No Keyboard
OpenBoot 3.27, 192 MB (60 ns) memory installed, Serial #10501480.
Ethernet address 8:0:20:a0:3d:68, Host ID: 80a03d68.

Rebooting with command: boot net:dhcp - install
Boot device: /pci@1f,0/pci@1,1/network@1,1:dhcp  File and args: -
install
TFTP Error: Access violation
Evaluating: boot net:dhcp - install

Boot load failed
```

The following is the snoop output of the network traffic seen during this failed installation attempt.

```
gw# snoop -d qe0 8:0:20:a0:3d:68
Using device /dev/qe (promiscuous mode)
OLD-BROADCAST -> BROADCAST    DHCP/BOOTP DHCPDISCOVER
dhcp01 -> client01  ICMP Echo request (ID: 9 Sequence number: 0)
dhcp01 -> client01  ICMP Echo request (ID: 9 Sequence number: 1)
gw-qe0 -> client01  DHCP/BOOTP DHCPOFFER
OLD-BROADCAST -> BROADCAST    DHCP/BOOTP DHCPREQUEST
gw-qe0 -> client01  DHCP/BOOTP DHCPACK
OLD-BROADCAST -> (broadcast)  ARP C Who is 192.168.250.20, client01 ?
client01 -> client01  ARP R 192.168.250.20, client01 is 8:0:20:a0:3d:68
client01 -> (broadcast)  ARP C Who is 192.168.250.10, gw-qe0 ?
gw-qe0 -> client01  ARP R 192.168.250.10, gw-qe0 is 8:0:20:7b:d9:e0
client01 -> install01 TFTP Read "SUNW.Ultra-5_10" (octet)
install01 -> client01  TFTP Error: access violation
```

An access error was encountered by client01 when attempting to download its boot image from the JumpStart installation server, install01. The client client01, was attempting to access the file SUNW.Ultra-5_10, which was *not* available on the install01. We resolved the issue by creating a symbolic link from SUNW.Ultra-5_10 to inetboot.SUN4U.Solaris_8-1 on install01 in the /tftpboot directory with the following commands:

```
install01# pwd
/tftpboot
install01# ln -s ./inetboot.SUN4U.Solaris_8-1 ./SUNW.Ultra-5_10
```

This resolved the JumpStart software error by creating a file /tftpboot/SUNW.Ultra-5_10 that pointed to the JumpStart miniroot image in the following manner:

```
install01# ls -l SUNW*
lrwxrwxrwx 1 root other 26 Feb 14 13:05 SUNW.Ultra-5_10 ->
inetboot.SUN4U.Solaris_8-1
```

With this step completed, the JumpStart software installation proceeded as described in "Installing the Client" on page 117.

Installing the Client

Once the DHPC server is configured properly and the `add_install_client` command ran on the install server, boot the client off of the network, using DHCP with the following command:

```
ok boot net:dhcp - install
Resetting ...

Sun Ultra 5/10 UPA/PCI (UltraSPARC-IIi 270MHz), No Keyboard
OpenBoot 3.27, 192 MB (60 ns) memory installed, Serial #10501480.
Ethernet address 8:0:20:a0:3d:68, Host ID: 80a03d68.

Rebooting with command: boot net:dhcp - install
Boot device: /pci@1f,0/pci@1,1/network@1,1:dhcp  File and args: -
install
SunOS Release 5.8 Version Generic_108528-07 64-bit
Copyright 1983-2001 Sun Microsystems, Inc.  All rights reserved.
Configuring /dev and /devices
Using DHCP for network configuration information.
Using sysid configuration file
192.168.252.11:/jumpstart/Sysidcfg/Solaris_8/sysidcfg
The system is coming up.  Please wait.
Starting remote procedure call (RPC) services: sysidns done.
Starting Solaris installation program...
Searching for JumpStart directory...
Using rules.ok from install01:/jumpstart.
Checking rules.ok file...
Using profile: entire-distribution.profile
Executing JumpStart preinstall phase...
Searching for SolStart directory...
Checking rules.ok file...
Using begin script: install_begin
Using finish script: patch_finish
Executing SolStart preinstall phase...
Executing begin script "install_begin"...
Begin script install_begin execution completed.
```

`sysidcfg` File Repository

The examples in this section assume that all JumpStart servers (boot01, config01, and instal101) are being used and that none of the servers are using any name service. The test systems are, in fact, using the /etc/nsswitch.files file with no modifications.

At this point the JumpStart client installation begins. Add the client to boot01 in the following manner:

```
boot01# ./add_install_client \
-s instal101:/jumpstart/OS/Solaris_8_2001-04 \
-c instal101:/jumpstart \
-i 192.168.250.20 \
-e 8:0:20:a0:3d:68 \
-p config01:/jumpstart/Sysidcfg/Solaris_8 client01 sun4u
```

Use the following `sysidcfg` file to automate the JumpStart software installation:

```
system_locale=en_US
timezone=US/Eastern
network_interface=primary {hostname=client01
                           ip_address=192.168.250.20
                           netmask=255.255.255.0
                           protocol_ipv6=no}
terminal=vt100
root_password=jPxa1fICIVZI6
security_policy=NONE
name_service=NONE
timeserver=localhost
```

When this information is provided, a JumpStart software installation produces the following output:

```
ok boot net - install
Resetting ...

Sun Ultra 5/10 UPA/PCI (UltraSPARC-IIi 270MHz), No Keyboard
OpenBoot 3.11, 192 MB memory installed, Serial #10501480.
Ethernet address 8:0:20:a0:3d:68, Host ID: 80a03d68.

Rebooting with command: boot net - install
Boot device: /pci@1f,0/pci@1,1/network@1,1  File and args: -
install
SunOS Release 5.8 Version Generic_108528-07 64-bit
Copyright 1983-2001 Sun Microsystems, Inc.  All rights reserved.
whoami: no domain name
Configuring /dev and /devices
Using RPC Bootparams for network configuration information.
Configured interface hme0
Using sysid configuration file
192.168.252.11:/jumpstart/Sysidcfg/Solaris_8/sysidcfg
The system is coming up.  Please wait.
Starting remote procedure call (RPC) services: sysidns done.
Starting Solaris installation program...
Searching for JumpStart directory...
Using rules.ok from 192.168.251.11:/jumpstart.
Checking rules.ok file...
Using profile: Profiles/entire-distribution.profile
Executing JumpStart preinstall phase...
Searching for SolStart directory...
Checking rules.ok file...
Using begin script: install_begin
Using finish script: patch_finish
Executing SolStart preinstall phase...
Executing begin script "install_begin"...
Begin script install_begin execution completed.
```

Diskette Repository

Sometimes, it is necessary to install a system before it is connected to a network. Alternatively, depending on how many systems require installation, it may not be convenient or possible to set up a JumpStart boot server. Depending on how many systems must be installed, the best alternative can be to install these systems automatically and not perform interactive Solaris OE installations on each of them.

It is possible to do this with JumpStart technology without taking the time and resources to build JumpStart boot, install, and configuration servers. Through the use of what is referred to as a profile diskette, you can JumpStart a Solaris OE system using only an internal diskette and CD-ROM drives. The profile diskette holds the JumpStart clients' rules file, any references to profiles, and the begin and finish scripts.

When the boot cdrom - install command is issued to the JumpStart client, the system automatically searches for the sysidcfg and the rules.ok files in the root directory of the internal diskette drive. If these files are present, then they are executed in the same fashion as the network-based installations.

Create this diskette with the following steps.

First, format an unformatted 1.4-Mbyte diskette with the following commands:

```
install01# fdformat -U
Formatting 1.44 MB in /vol/dev/rdiskette0/unnamed_floppy
Press return to start formatting floppy.
.................................................................
................
install01# newfs /vol/dev/diskette0/unnamed_floppy
newfs: construct a new filesystem
/vol/dev/rdiskette0/unnamed_floppy: (y/n)? y
/vol/dev/rdiskette0/unnamed_floppy:      2880 sectors in 80
cylinders of 2 tracks, 18 sectors
        1.4MB in 5 cyl groups (16 c/g, 0.28MB/g, 128 i/g)
super-block backups (for fsck -F ufs -o b=#) at:
 32, 640, 1184, 1792, 2336,
```

Note – To avoid formatting or read errors, it is recommended that a new or previously unused diskette be used.

Use the following `rules` file to generate a `rules.ok` file, then copy it to the diskette.

```
hostname client01 - Profiles/entire-distribution.profile -
```

Use the following `sysidcfg` file to automate the JumpStart installation.

```
system_locale=en_US
timezone=US/Eastern
network_interface=primary {hostname=client01
                           ip_address=192.168.250.20
                           netmask=255.255.255.0
                           protocol_ipv6=no}
terminal=vt100
root_password=jPxa1fICIVZI6
security_policy=NONE
name_service=NONE
timeserver=localhost
```

Next, copy a `rules.ok` file, appropriate for the JumpStart software to be installed, on to the diskette. For this example, the diskette has the following contents:

```
install01# pwd
/floppy/unnamed_floppy
install01# find . -print
.
./rules.ok
./check
./sysidcfg
./rules
./Profiles
./Profiles/entire-distribution.profile
```

Once the JumpStart profile diskette is inserted into the diskette drive of client01 along with Solaris 8 OE 1 or 2 Software CD, the installation of client01 begins with the following command:

```
ok boot cdrom - install
```

With this provided information, a JumpStart software installation produces the following output.

```
ok boot net - install
Resetting ...

Sun Ultra 5/10 UPA/PCI (UltraSPARC-IIi 270MHz), No Keyboard
OpenBoot 3.11, 192 MB memory installed, Serial #10501480.
Ethernet address 8:0:20:a0:3d:68, Host ID: 80a03d68.

Rebooting with command: boot cdrom - install
Boot device: /pci@1f,0/pci@1,1/ide@3/cdrom@2,0:f  File and args:
- install
SunOS Release 5.8 Version Generic_108528-07 64-bit
Copyright 1983-2001 Sun Microsystems, Inc.  All rights reserved.
Configuring /dev and /devices
Using RPC Bootparams for network configuration information.
Skipping interface hme0
Using sysid configuration file from local floppy
The system is coming up.  Please wait.
Starting remote procedure call (RPC) services: sysidns done.
Starting Solaris installation program...
Searching for JumpStart directory...
rules.ok found on floppy.
Copying information to disk...
Using rules.ok from floppy.
Checking rules.ok file...
Using profile: Profiles/entire-distribution.profile
Executing JumpStart preinstall phase...
Searching for SolStart directory...
Checking rules.ok file...
Using begin script: install_begin
Using finish script: patch_finish
Executing SolStart preinstall phase...
Executing begin script "install_begin"...
Begin script install_begin execution completed.
```

Summary

This chapter documented JumpStart technology automation with all currently available technologies:

- NIS
- NIS+
- DHCP
- `sysidcfg` file
- Diskettes

For each of the mechanisms, we described the procedures needed to automate a JumpStart software installation. In addition, we also looked at the lab environment in which these procedures were performed.

## CHAPTER 6

JumpStart Internals

This chapter applies the concepts presented in Chapter 2, "JumpStart Overview" and Chapter 3, "JumpStart Customizations" to a SPARC-based automated JumpStart software installation by looking at the sequence of network traffic generated.

The JumpStart technology process is divided into three phases, based on the network protocols encountered.

1. The first phase of the boot process is implemented in the client's OpenBoot PROM (OBP) and involves the JumpStart boot client's initial boot and its acquisition of an IP address based on the client's MAC address.

2. The second phase begins as the system boots the miniroot and continues with an automated installation.

3. The third phase continues the automated installation as the installation client mounts the root directory of the JumpStart server and processes the `rules.ok` file.

To illustrate what happens during installation, we detail in this chapter an automated JumpStart installation, using the same network used in Chapter 5, "Automating Installations." We use `sysidcfg` files to automate the installation, and we use RARP instead of DHCP. See FIGURE 6-1, FIGURE 6-2, and FIGURE 6-3 for flowcharts illustrating the process.

The information in this chapter is intended as a reference and can be useful in troubleshooting and debugging your JumpStart environment. To further detail how the installation works, use the Solaris OE utility `snoop` to capture and examine the network traffic generated during a JumpStart software installation.

Phase One

To begin an automated JumpStart installation, the client's OBP implements the boot process and involves the JumpStart boot client's initial boot. FIGURE 6-1 illustrates phase one.

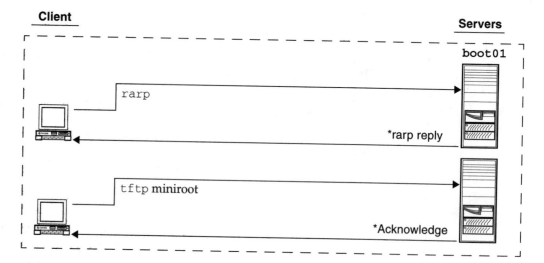

FIGURE 6-1   Phase One

1. The client, client01, obtains an IP address for the JumpStart client.

   Here is an illustration of the initial RARP traffic from client01 to boot01:

```
   1   0.00000 OLD-BROADCAST -> (broadcast)  length:   64  RARP C
Who is 8:0:20:a0:3d:68 ?
   2   0.00523 192.168.250.11 -> 192.168.250.20 length:   60  RARP
R 8:0:20:a0:3d:68 is 192.168.250.20, 192.168.250.20
```

2. After the JumpStart client has its IP address, it asks to download the appropriate miniroot from this IP address.

Here is an example of the network traffic.

```
   3   0.00262 192.168.250.20 -> 192.168.250.11 length:   64  TFTP
Read "C0A8FA14" (octet)
   4   0.16681 192.168.250.11 -> 192.168.250.20 length:  558  TFTP
Data block 1 (512 bytes)
   5   0.00665 192.168.250.20 -> 192.168.250.11 length:   64  TFTP
Ack  block 1
   6   0.00134 192.168.250.11 -> 192.168.250.20 length:  558  TFTP
Data block 2 (512 bytes)
   7   0.00886 192.168.250.20 -> 192.168.250.11 length:   64  TFTP
Ack  block 2
   8   0.00124 192.168.250.11 -> 192.168.250.20 length:  558  TFTP
Data block 3 (512 bytes)
[...]
 622   0.00112 192.168.250.11 -> 192.168.250.20 length:  430  TFTP
Data block 310 (384 bytes) (last block)
 623   0.00459 192.168.250.20 -> 192.168.250.11 length:   64  TFTP
Ack  block 310
```

3. The system then boots and the miniroot is loaded.

This miniroot is neither architecture-specific nor model-specific. It is designed to bring up a generic Sun Solaris OE system, based on a specific kernel architecture but with an unknown hardware configuration, to a minimum OS level. The miniroot must support all Solaris OE-supported hardware to permit installation tasks. The miniroot kernel is platform specific. For instance, there is one miniroot for all sun4u Solaris 8 OE JumpStart clients. This kernel must contain enough information about potential hardware configuration to be able to bring up all sun4u systems, from an Ultra 5 workstation to an Ultra Enterprise 4500 kernel architecture to a Sun Fire 6800 server, as far as the point where a Solaris OE installation can begin.

This set of diverse requirements and limits on the size of the miniroot, which is only 158,592 bytes for Solaris 8 OE sun4u JumpStart clients, forces the implementation of many workarounds and shortcuts. Many of the workarounds center on the software switch mechanism, uname -m, and the requirements to provide Solaris OE features in an architecturally neutral way. For additional details on the miniroot, see Chapter 9, "Customizing JumpStart Framework for Installation and Recovery."

Phase Two

At this point, the IP address has been obtained and the installation client has been booted with the downloaded miniroot. The second level of the boot process begins with the JumpStart client requesting boot parameters from a JumpStart server. FIGURE 6-2 illustrates the flow of phase two.

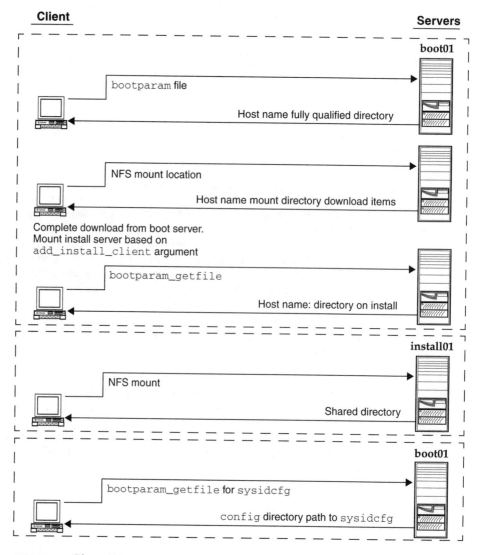

FIGURE 6-2   Phase Two

1. The JumpStart server provides the requested boot parameters (from `/etc/bootparams`) to the installation client, `client01`. This information specifies the client's root filesystem on the boot server.

2. The JumpStart client, `client01`, uses this information to NFS-mount the specified directory as its root filesystem.

Example of the downloaded additional information:

```
624    2.36541 OLD-BROADCAST -> (broadcast)  length:    64  RARP C
Who is 8:0:20:a0:3d:68 ?
625    0.00457 192.168.250.11 -> 192.168.250.20 length:    60  RARP
R 8:0:20:a0:3d:68 is 192.168.250.20, 192.168.250.20
626    0.00287 192.168.250.20 -> BROADCAST    length:  118  BPARAM
C WHOAMI? 192.168.250.20
627    0.01685 192.168.250.11 -> 192.168.250.20 length:  114  BPARAM
R WHOAMI? client01 in
628    0.01174 192.168.250.20 -> (broadcast)  length:    64  ARP C
Who is 192.168.250.11, 192.168.250.11 ?
629    0.00037 192.168.250.11 -> 192.168.250.20 length:    60  ARP
R 192.168.250.11, 192.168.250.11 is 8:0:20:1d:83:a8
630    0.00515 192.168.250.20 -> 192.168.250.11 length:  106  BPARAM
C GETFILE root
631    0.00307 192.168.250.11 -> 192.168.250.20 length:  162  BPARAM
R GETFILE File=/jumpstart/OS/Solaris_8_2001-
04/Solaris_8/Tools/Boot
632    0.01265 192.168.250.20 -> 192.168.250.11 length:    98
PORTMAP C GETPORT prog=100005 (MOUNT) vers=1 proto=UDP
633    0.00284 192.168.250.11 -> 192.168.250.20 length:    70
PORTMAP R GETPORT port=32781
634    0.01261 192.168.250.20 -> 192.168.250.11 length:  178  MOUNT1
C Mount /jumpstart/OS/Solaris_8_2001-04/Solaris_8/Tools/Boot
635    0.00781 192.168.250.11 -> 192.168.250.20 length:  102  MOUNT1
R Mount OK FH=8DDA
636    0.01274 192.168.250.20 -> 192.168.250.11 length:  162  NFS
C LOOKUP2 FH=8DDA platform
637    0.00108 192.168.250.11 -> 192.168.250.20 length:  170  NFS
R LOOKUP2 OK FH=9962
[...]
```

3. The JumpStart client mounts `install01` when it requires more of the Solaris OE image than is installed on the boot server installation, `boot01`.

The next significant network packet in the snoop trace is packet 15687. `boot01` provides `client01` with the IP address of `install01`. The packet looks like this:

```
ETHER:   ----- Ether Header -----
ETHER:
ETHER:   Packet 15687 arrived at 15:06:34.10
ETHER:   Packet size = 150 bytes
ETHER:   Destination = 8:0:20:a0:3d:68, Sun
ETHER:   Source      = 8:0:20:1d:83:a8, Sun
ETHER:   Ethertype = 0800 (IP)
ETHER:
[...]
IP:    Source address = 192.168.250.11, 192.168.250.11
IP:    Destination address = 192.168.250.20, 192.168.250.20
IP:    No options
IP:
UDP:   ----- UDP Header -----
UDP:
UDP:   Source port = 32771
UDP:   Destination port = 32770 (Sun RPC)
UDP:   Length = 116
UDP:   Checksum = DFC7
UDP:
[...]
BPARAM:   ----- Boot Parameters -----
BPARAM:
BPARAM:   Proc = 2 (Get file name)
BPARAM:   Server name = install01
BPARAM:   Server addr = 192.168.251.11 (192.168.251.11)
BPARAM:   Server file = /jumpstart/OS/Solaris_8_2001-04
BPARAM:
```

The actual NFS mount from install01 doesn't occur until packet 15740. At that point, the /jumpstart/OS/Solaris_8_2001-04 directory is mounted and client01 begins to download information directly from that server. The snoop trace appears as follows:

```
15740    0.00085 192.168.250.20 -> 192.168.251.11 length:    98
PORTMAP C GETPORT prog=100005 (MOUNT) vers=3 proto=UDP
15741    0.00406 192.168.251.11 -> 192.168.250.20 length:    70
PORTMAP R GETPORT port=32781
15742    0.00100 192.168.250.20 -> 192.168.251.11 length:    82
MOUNT3 C Null
15743    0.00176 192.168.251.11 -> 192.168.250.20 length:    66
MOUNT3 R Null
15744    0.00242 192.168.250.20 -> 192.168.251.11 length:   154
MOUNT3 C Mount /jumpstart/OS/Solaris_8_2001-04
15745    0.00862 192.168.251.11 -> 192.168.250.20 length:   114
MOUNT3 R Mount OK FH=C9EC Auth=unix
```

4. The JumpStart software installation is determining the configuration of the system. To complete the configuration of client01, since this installation is based on sysidcfg files, client01 issues the following BPARAM request.

```
16226    0.04771 192.168.250.20 -> 192.168.250.255 length:   162
BPARAM C GETFILE sysid_config
```

This request is answered by boot01 and the following packet, which includes the server IP address, name, and the location of the sysidcfg file.

```
ETHER:    ----- Ether Header -----
ETHER:
ETHER:    Packet 16227 arrived at 15:06:39.71
ETHER:    Packet size = 146 bytes
ETHER:    Destination = 8:0:20:a0:3d:68, Sun
ETHER:    Source      = 8:0:20:1d:83:a8, Sun
[...]
BPARAM:   ----- Boot Parameters -----
BPARAM:
BPARAM:   Proc = 2 (Get file name)
BPARAM:   Server name = config01
BPARAM:   Server addr = 192.168.252.11 (192.168.252.11)
BPARAM:   Server file = /jumpstart/Sysidcfg/Solaris_8
```

5. This packet, number 16227, tells client01 to find the sysid_config file on config01 in the /jumpstart/sysidcfg/Solaris_8 directory.

6. `client01` then performs the necessary portmapper and NFS mount activities to mount and download the `sysidcfg` file from `config01`.

```
16228    0.03776 192.168.250.20 -> 192.168.252.11 length:    98
PORTMAP C GETPORT prog=100005 (MOUNT) vers=3 proto=UDP
16229    0.00184 192.168.250.20 -> 192.168.250.11 length:    60   TCP
D=2049 S=1023      Ack=331427137 Seq=2125310 Len=0 Win=24820
16230    0.00179 192.168.252.11 -> 192.168.250.20 length:    70
PORTMAP R GETPORT port=32781
16231    0.00097 192.168.250.20 -> 192.168.252.11 length:    82
MOUNT3 C Null
16232    0.00176 192.168.252.11 -> 192.168.250.20 length:    66
MOUNT3 R Null
16233    0.00240 192.168.250.20 -> 192.168.252.11 length:    150
MOUNT3 C Mount /jumpstart/Sysidcfg/Solaris_8
16234    0.00752 192.168.252.11 -> 192.168.250.20 length:    114
MOUNT3 R Mount OK FH=16FC Auth=unix
16235    0.00708 192.168.250.20 -> 192.168.252.11 length:    98
PORTMAP C GETPORT prog=100003 (NFS) vers=3 proto=TCP
16236    0.00290 192.168.252.11 -> 192.168.250.20 length:    70
PORTMAP R GETPORT port=2049
16237    0.00373 192.168.250.20 -> 192.168.252.11 length:    62   TCP
D=2049 S=32769 Syn Seq=13921734 Len=0 Win=24820
Options=<nop,nop,sackOK,mss 1460>
16238    0.00110 192.168.252.11 -> 192.168.250.20 length:    62   TCP
D=32769 S=2049 Syn Ack=13921735 Seq=381419211 Len=0 Win=24820
Options=<nop,nop,sackOK,mss 1460>
16239    0.00060 192.168.250.20 -> 192.168.252.11 length:    60   TCP
D=2049 S=32769      Ack=381419212 Seq=13921735 Len=0 Win=24820
16240    0.00092 192.168.250.20 -> 192.168.252.11 length:    130  NFS
C NULL3
16241    0.00077 192.168.252.11 -> 192.168.250.20 length:    54   TCP
D=32769 S=2049      Ack=13921811 Seq=381419212 Len=0 Win=24744
```

7. When the search for the `config01` system and mounting are performed, the following messages are displayed on the console of the JumpStart `client01`.

```
Using sysid configuration file
192.168.252.11:/jumpstart/Sysidcfg/Solaris_8/sysidcfg
```

Phase Three

This level of the boot process continues with the automated installation. The next set of messages displayed on the console of the JumpStart client indicates that the custom JumpStart software installation is about to begin.

```
Searching for JumpStart directory...
Using rules.ok from 192.168.251.11:/jumpstart.
Checking rules.ok file...
```

FIGURE 6-3 illustrates the flow of phase three.

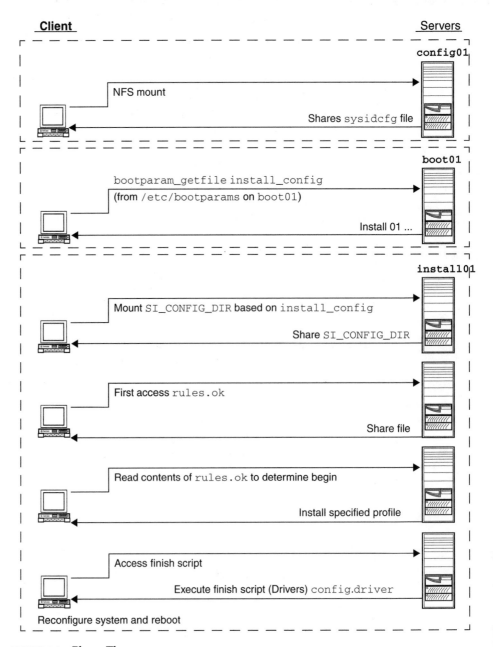

Client   **Servers**

config01

NFS mount

Shares `sysidcfg` file

boot01

`bootparam_getfile install_config`

(from `/etc/bootparams` on `boot01`)

Install 01 ...

install01

Mount `SI_CONFIG_DIR` based on `install_config`

Share `SI_CONFIG_DIR`

First access `rules.ok`

Share file

Read contents of `rules.ok` to determine begin

Install specified profile

Access finish script

Execute finish script (Drivers) `config.driver`

Reconfigure system and reboot

FIGURE 6-3 Phase Three

1. The first step in this installation is the attempt by the JumpStart client to access the `install_config` file by issuing a BPARAM request as follows.

```
ETHER:   ----- Ether Header -----
ETHER:
ETHER:   Packet 31856 arrived at 15:07:51.68
ETHER:   Packet size = 166 bytes
ETHER:   Destination = ff:ff:ff:ff:ff:ff, (broadcast)
ETHER:   Source      = 8:0:20:a0:3d:68, Sun
ETHER:   Ethertype = 0800 (IP)
ETHER:
[...]
BPARAM:  ----- Boot Parameters -----
BPARAM:
BPARAM:  Proc = 2 (Get file name)
BPARAM:  Hostname = client01
BPARAM:  File = install_config
BPARAM:
```

This request is answered by `boot01` in accordance with its `/etc/bootparams` file, and `boot01` points the JumpStart client to `install01`.

2. The JumpStart client is then told to mount the `/jumpstart` directory on `install01` and search for the needed information.

```
ETHER:   ----- Ether Header -----
ETHER:
ETHER:   Packet 31857 arrived at 15:07:51.70
ETHER:   Packet size = 126 bytes
ETHER:   Destination = 8:0:20:a0:3d:68, Sun
ETHER:   Source      = 8:0:20:1d:83:a8, Sun
ETHER:   Ethertype = 0800 (IP)
ETHER:
[...]
BPARAM:  ----- Boot Parameters -----
BPARAM:
BPARAM:  Proc = 2 (Get file name)
BPARAM:  Server name = install01
BPARAM:  Server addr = 192.168.251.11 (192.168.251.11)
BPARAM:  Server file = /jumpstart
BPARAM:
```

3. The next sequence of information the JumpStart client needs is the `rules.ok` file. It first mounts the `/jumpstart` directory from `install01` as illustrated.

```
31857    0.01183 192.168.250.11 -> 192.168.250.20 length:  126
BPARAM R GETFILE File=/jumpstart
31858    0.04321 192.168.250.20 -> 192.168.251.11 length:   98
PORTMAP C GETPORT prog=100005 (MOUNT) vers=3 proto=UDP
31859    0.00381 192.168.251.11 -> 192.168.250.20 length:   70
PORTMAP R GETPORT port=32781
31860    0.00100 192.168.250.20 -> 192.168.251.11 length:   82
MOUNT3 C Null
31861    0.00327 192.168.251.11 -> 192.168.250.20 length:   66
MOUNT3 R Null
31862    0.00239 192.168.250.20 -> 192.168.251.11 length:  130
MOUNT3 C Mount /jumpstart
31863    0.00699 192.168.251.11 -> 192.168.250.20 length:  114
MOUNT3 R Mount OK FH=008A Auth=unix
31864    0.00694 192.168.250.20 -> 192.168.251.11 length:   98
PORTMAP C GETPORT prog=100003 (NFS) vers=3 proto=TCP
31865    0.00293 192.168.251.11 -> 192.168.250.20 length:   70
PORTMAP R GETPORT port=2049
```

4. The JumpStart client searches for the file on `install01`.

```
ETHER:  ----- Ether Header -----
ETHER:
ETHER:  Packet 31879 arrived at 15:07:51.80
ETHER:  Packet size = 178 bytes
ETHER:  Destination = 8:0:20:7b:d9:e0, Sun
ETHER:  Source      = 8:0:20:a0:3d:68, Sun
ETHER:  Ethertype = 0800 (IP)
ETHER:
[...]
NFS:  ----- Sun NFS -----
NFS:
NFS:  Proc = 3 (Look up file name)
NFS:  File handle = [008A]
NFS:
0080000800000002000A0000000000024C5B1615000A0000000000024C5B1615
NFS:  File name = rules.ok
NFS:
```

This particular `rules.ok` file specifies the following file for `client01`.

```
hostname client01 - entire-distribution.profile Drivers/config.driver
```

This rule tells JumpStart software to use `entire-distribution.profile` to specify the type of Solaris OE installation, disk layout, and any additional packages that need to be installed on the system. The contents of `entire-distribution.profile` are as follows.

```
install_type    initial_install
cluster         SUNWCall
partitioning    explicit
filesys         rootdisk.s1    100     swap
filesys         rootdisk.s0    free    /
system_type     standalone
```

Refer to "Profiles" on page 40 of Chapter 3 for detailed descriptions of these profile options.

Once the contents of the provided profile (`entire-distribution.profile`) have been parsed and the following message is displayed to the console of the JumpStart server, the JumpStart client acknowledges that it is using `entire-distribution.profile` to define the Solaris OE installation.

```
Using profile: entire-distribution.profile
Executing JumpStart preinstall phase...
Searching for SolStart directory...
Checking rules.ok file...
```

5. The JumpStart software installation then determines what, if any, begin scripts are specified by the `rules.ok` file.

In this example, no begin scripts are specified. Note the minus character (-) in the rules begin script entry. The JumpStart client displays the following messages to the console to indicate that it is running the `install_begin` and `patch_finish` scripts. Both of these scripts are part of the JumpStart framework and can be considered placeholders for user-specified begin and finish scripts. They are run during every automated JumpStart software installation, regardless of whether begin or finish scripts are specified in the `rules.ok` file.

```
Using begin script: install_begin
Using finish script: patch_finish
```

6. If there are begin scripts in the preinstallation phase, they are executed now.

   The following messages indicate that no custom begin scripts were executed in this particular example.

```
Executing SolStart preinstall phase...
Executing begin script "install_begin"...
Begin script install_begin execution completed.
```

7. The system continues to implement the contents of the `entire-distribution.profile` configuration file.

   The following is an example of the console output of this step.

```
Processing default locales
        - Specifying default locale (en_US)

Processing profile
        - Selecting cluster (SUNWCall)
        - Selecting locale (en_US)

Installing 64 bit Solaris packages
        - Selecting all disks
        - Configuring boot device
        - Using disk (c0t0d0) for "rootdisk"
        - Configuring swap (c0t0d0s1)
        - Configuring / (c0t0d0s0)

Verifying disk configuration

Verifying space allocation
        - Total software size:   737.47 Mbytes

Preparing system for Solaris install

Configuring disk (c0t0d0)
        - Creating Solaris disk label (VTOC)

Creating and checking UFS filesystems
        - Creating / (c0t0d0s0)
```

8. At this point, the JumpStart client, `client01`, is ready to start installing the Solaris OE software onto its formatted and partitioned disk.

This installation generates a tremendous amount of NFS traffic between client01 and install01. The console output from client01 looks like the following.

```
Starting software installation
        SUNWxwrtx...done.   737.43 Mbytes remaining.
        SUNWxwrtl...done.   737.38 Mbytes remaining.
        SUNWxwhl....done.   737.36 Mbytes remaining.
        SUNWwbapi...done.   736.85 Mbytes remaining.
        SUNWulocf...done.   736.76 Mbytes remaining.
        SUNWulcfx...done.   736.71 Mbytes remaining.
        SUNWulcf....done.   733.04 Mbytes remaining.
[...]
```

9. Once the software installation is complete, the system executes the finish script specified by the rules.ok file.

In this case, no finish scripts were specified, so the system completes its installation and performs an automatic system reboot.

The installation of the profile-specified information has been successfully completed when the following message is displayed to the console of the JumpStart client.

```
Completed software installation

Solaris 8 software installation succeeded
```

10. The JumpStart software installation modifies system configuration files as needed. This includes modifications to the /etc/vfstab, /etc/hosts, and files that are specified below.

```
Customizing system files
        - Mount points table (/etc/vfstab)
        - Network host addresses (/etc/hosts)

Customizing system devices
        - Physical devices (/devices)
        - Logical devices (/dev)
```

11. The configuration of the appropriate boot information begins on the newly installed boot disk.

```
Installing boot information
        - Installing boot blocks (c0t0d0s0)
```

12. A message reminding the administrator where the JumpStart software installation logs are stored is generated.

```
Installation log location
        - /a/var/sadm/system/logs/install_log (before reboot)
        - /var/sadm/system/logs/install_log (after reboot)

Installation complete
```

13. At this point, the system moves into the postinstallation phase.

   The first script is the Solaris OE patch_finish script.

```
Executing SolStart postinstall phase...
Executing finish script "patch_finish"...

Finish script patch_finish execution completed.
```

14. Any finish scripts or driver scripts listed in the rules.ok file are executed.

   This particular rules.ok file specifies that the finish script, config.driver, be executed. The console output is as follows:

```
Executing JumpStart postinstall phase...
Executing finish script "Drivers/config.driver"...
[...]
```

15. The contents of the finish script are executed.

This completes the JumpStart software installation process. The system reboots after printing one final reminder about where the logs are located.

```
The begin script log 'begin.log'
is located in /var/sadm/system/logs after reboot.

The finish script log 'finish.log'
is located in /var/sadm/system/logs after reboot.

syncing filesystems... done
rebooting...
Resetting ...
```

Summary

This chapter detailed step-by-step directions of the three phases of a successful automated JumpStart software installation. The network used in this example was the same as the network used in Chapter 5, "Automating Installations." The chapter illustrated how network traffic was generated and associated the details about how the network traffic with the console output of the JumpStart client.

## CHAPTER 7

JumpStart Security

The use of JumpStart software in environments where security is a concern has always been challenging. The difficulty arises from the protocols and authentication mechanisms used during JumpStart installations. UNIX® protocols potentially used during JumpStart software installations include TFTP, RARP, BOOT Parameters (BOOTP), Network File System (NFS), and HTTP. During a JumpStart installation, none of these protocols use any available encryption or strong authentication. The only authentication methods performed during a JumpStart installation are the MAC address of the client or the corresponding IP address. Both of these methods of authentication can easily be spoofed.

These issues have forced architects and administrators to find alternative methods to protect their JumpStart environments against unauthorized access. There are two types of unauthorized access: unauthorized JumpStart installation of clients and unauthorized access of JumpStart-provided information.

This chapter evaluates and recommends alternatives for securing a JumpStart environment. See the following sections for details.

- Demand-only connection
- Physical cable connection: air gap
- Limitations on JumpStart services
- JumpStart server hardening
- Network segmentation
- Access control

Note – For any of the following recommendations to be successful, well-defined policies and procedures must be in place. Without them, your environment cannot take full advantage of a secured JumpStart environment.

Demand-Only Connection

One of the simplest ways to protect against the unauthorized JumpStart installation of a server is to add a JumpStart client into the JumpStart environment *only* when it is actively being installed. By making sure the JumpStart installation entries are removed when the installation is complete, you can avoid accidental and unauthorized JumpStart software installations.

This method is easily maintained in a lights-out environment. Just add the client to the JumpStart environment with the `add_install_client` command and remove the client from this environment with the `rm_install_client` command.

For this installation-only connection solution to be effective, procedures and policies must be strictly adhered to in your datacenter so that systems can quickly and effectively be added to and removed from the JumpStart environment. One common technique to simplify the implementation of this recommendation is to maintain a list of JumpStart client information, separate from the JumpStart infrastructure, to provide easy access in emergency situations such as system recovery.

Note – When staging a system, keep in mind that the client's system identification information must be modified to reflect its production information. See `sys-unconfig`(1M) for details on changing a system's identification.

Physical Cable Connection: Air Gap

One of the most secure mechanisms to restrict JumpStart server access is an "air gap." The security for this mechanism comes from the absence of a physical cable connection between the JumpStart environment and the client. The JumpStart server should have a minimum of two network connections. These connections are the primary and the air gap: the primary is always attached to a network, whereas the air gap is connected only when necessary. This security mechanism also requires strict adherence to procedures and policies of your datacenter.

An air gap prevents accidental JumpStart installations and unauthorized access in the JumpStart network. You just plug the JumpStart client into an isolated JumpStart network or JumpStart server to install the client and then unplug it when the installation is complete.

This solution is frequently implemented in datacenter environments by means of a physically separated JumpStart segment that is connected to the JumpStart client only when an installation is required. The cables used to connect to the JumpStart network should have different and easily recognizable colors or markings, to ensure that they are not accidently left plugged in.

The air-gap mechanism is extremely useful in environments where there is a separate build-out or staging environment. In this type of environment, systems are prebuilt before being moved to their appropriate location in the network. Once these systems are moved to their final location, they are only plugged in to the appropriate production network segments.

The air-gap solution isn't for datacenter environments that do not have onsite staff. The reason is that in the case of a system recovery, human intervention is required for the physical reconnection of the cable to restart the JumpStart client.

Limitation on JumpStart Services

A successful JumpStart installation depends on a variety of services. These services are detailed in Chapter 2, "JumpStart Overview," in Chapter 5, "Automating Installations," and in particular, in Chapter 6, "JumpStart Internals."

One effective mechanism to limit client access to JumpStart services is to use the rm_install_client command on the JumpStart server to prevent the client from accessing JumpStart services. This procedure, which is described in "Demand-Only Connection" on page 144, also helps prevent accidental JumpStart installations.

Another solution to secure the JumpStart environment is to restrict access to the information provided by JumpStart services. For example, you can disable NFS export of the JumpStart installation server filesystems when NFS is not in use. You can disable other JumpStart-specific services by commenting them out of /etc/inetd.conf or by stopping daemons, on each JumpStart server. For example, stop the NFS export on the installation and configuration servers and stop BOOTP and TFTP on the boot server.

Note – The specifics of limiting services in your JumpStart environment depend on the JumpStart architecture in your datacenter.

The major issue with this solution is that when any one particular system is actively being installed, any other system on the network can still gain access to the JumpStart services. Although the JumpStart infrastructure is protected most of the time because it is disabled, when in use it is vulnerable to unauthorized access. An unauthorized user only has to wait until the environment is in use to attack.

This option is most effective when used in conjunction with the other security alternatives detailed in this chapter.

JumpStart Server Hardening

As with any standard Solaris OE installation, a JumpStart server, by default, offers many services not essential for JumpStart software installations. Correspondingly, a strongly recommended security precaution with JumpStart infrastructures is to harden, or secure, a Solaris OE of the JumpStart server.

Only NFS, RPC, and TFTP services are required on a JumpStart server. All other services on the JumpStart server can be disabled. In addition, if separate configuration, installation, and boot JumpStart servers are used, then additional services can be disabled. The services required on each of these servers are listed in TABLE 7-1.

TABLE 7-1   Required Services for JumpStart Servers

JumpStart Servers	NFS	RPC	TFTP
Configuration	X	X	
Installation	X	X	
Boot	X	X	X

It is strongly recommended that administrator access to the JumpStart servers be performed over an encrypted connection. This is most commonly implemented through the use of Secure Shell (SSH). For additional information about SSH, see the opensource SSH web site at `http://www.ssh.org`.

These recommendations can also be implemented with the Solaris Security Toolkit described in Chapter 10, "Solaris Security Toolkit." A `jumpstart-hardening.driver` script is included with the Toolkit. This driver script performs all of the hardening tasks supported by the Toolkit in the `secure.driver` script, with the exception of `disable-nfs.fin` and `disable-rpc.fin`. One additional modification to the default Toolkit configuration is to *not* disable the TFTP service from `/etc/inetd.conf`. This service is only required on the boot server. NFS and RPC services are required on all JumpStart servers.

Network Segmentation

Network segmentation is a highly recommended mechanism to protect your JumpStart environment, particularly when used in combination with the other recommendations made in this chapter. Network segmentation doesn't provide all the security of the air-gap alternative, but it does allow JumpStart technology traffic to be isolated to only those systems and networks that require it.

By isolating the JumpStart technology traffic to only the required network segments, you dramatically increase the potential for misuse.

When you combine network segmentation with the removal of JumpStart clients from the JumpStart servers, see "Demand-Only Connection" on page 144, the potential for accidental or unauthorized JumpStart software installations is significantly reduced.

The idea behind this alternative is to have separate network segments dedicated to JumpStart technology traffic. These network segments provide JumpStart services to only those systems requiring it. With access restricted in this manner, the JumpStart infrastructure is considerably less exposed to security threats than if the services are available on all network segments within the environment.

Segmentation in N-Tier Architectures

This alternative is most easily deployed in N-Tier architectures where there are well-defined system types on each tier. In addition, N-Tier-based architectures permit the segmentation of JumpStart servers as well. For further security of these connections, each tier should be on a network segment separate from that of the other tiers and the JumpStart servers themselves. Harden the JumpStart server according to the directions in the "JumpStart Server Hardening" on page 146. By separating these network segments, you enforce relatively granular traffic flows. For additional details on N-Tier architectures, please refer to the Sun BluePrints Online article, "Building Secure N-Tier Environments," October 2000.

Segmentation in Gateway Systems

The different network segments can be connected through the use of gateway systems. These gateway systems function as JumpStart boot servers when RARP is used, or as BOOTP relays when DHC is used. In addition, these gateway machines also restrict network traffic to only the appropriate hosts. Ideally, these gateway systems implement the recommendations made in the following section and in "JumpStart Server Hardening" on page 146.

Access Control: Choke Points

Use a choke point, fireridge, or firewall to control access to the JumpStart infrastructure. Choke points can be implemented as separate gateway machines, or software can be installed on each of the JumpStart servers. In either case, choke points allow traffic flows to be restricted according to the type of traffic and source/destination ports.

This mechanism can be used in different ways to limit access to the JumpStart infrastructure. One alternative is to configure the choke points to disable all access to the JumpStart environment except when a particular system is being built. This enables the most restrictive configuration. Traffic is only permitted when required. A less restrictive alternative allows traffic, but only from JumpStart-built systems. This configuration is less secure because any of the JumpStart clients can still access the JumpStart infrastructure, but it is more restrictive than allowing full network access.

Using choke points to restrict JumpStart infrastructure access is most effective when done in conjunction with the network segmentation recommendations made in the "Network Segmentation" on page 147 and "JumpStart Server Hardening" on page 146. When used in combination, these complementing mechanisms provide a great deal of protection for the JumpStart infrastructure.

Summary

JumpStart environments can be secured and protected by several mechanisms, as detailed in this chapter. It is most important to note that the alternatives presented are not mutually exclusive. The most secure and appropriate alternative for your datacenter may be to use several mechanisms in conjunction. Although we recommend which alternatives are most effective, these recommendations greatly depend on your datacenter architecture. When considering which alternative is most appropriate, you should carefully consider the environment in which the solution is deployed.

Despite its potential security issues, JumpStart technology can and should be used in even the most secured environment for proper system installation and initial configuration.

In addition, the importance of appropriate policies and procedures regarding the use of JumpStart technology cannot be overstated. Without implemented and enforced documented policies and procedures, the overall security of the JumpStart environment, despite the recommendations implemented, will not fulfill the documented requirements.

## CHAPTER 8

WebStart Flash

The Solaris OE Flash installation component is introduced in Solaris 8 4/01 (Update 4) OE and extends JumpStart technology by adding a mechanism to create a system archive, a snapshot of an installed system, and installation of the Solaris OE from that archive. Flash, the new mechanism for installing the Solaris OE, enables the specification and creation of archive contents and servers. This chapter describes the following Flash topics:

- Overview
- Identifying the master machine
- Creating and administering archives
- Changing profile keywords or keyword values to support Flash
- Using Flash in a complete example installation

Overview

WebStart Flash provides a mechanism by which a specific or reference installation of the Solaris OE is archived. That archive can then be used to install the Solaris OE. The reference installation is created from the on-disk Solaris OE, which includes all installed software. This system is designated as the master machine. The reference installation can be a Solaris OE installed by any means, for example, with JumpStart software, from CD, or by an interactive installation.

After the master machine is identified, the reference installation is captured in a Flash archive. A central feature of Flash, this archive is essentially a point-in-time snapshot of the Solaris OE, software patches, and applications on the master machine.

The Flash extensions enable administrators to install the archive from an NFS server or an HTTP server, in addition to installing from a traditional JumpStart server. Additionally, the archive can be accessed from a disk device (including CD-ROM) or tape device local to the installation client. The Flash archive is transmitted over the network to the installation client and written to the disk. After the archive is written to the installation client's disk, any necessary archive modifications are performed.

For example, configuration files, such as /etc/nsswitch.conf, on the installation client may need to vary from the file on the master machine. The Flash mechanism enables automation of modifications and allows for differences in kernel architecture or device differences between the master machine and the installation client.

Additionally, Flash enables automatic resolution of partitioning differences between the master machine and the installation client. For example, if the Flash archive was created on a system with a single root (/) partition and the installation client has separate / and /var partitions, the Flash archive automatically customizes itself to the installation client. Remember, the installation client partitioning must be correctly specified in the JumpStart software profile.

The Flash archive is a snapshot of a system and, as such, includes all specified files on that system. If a Flash archive is created from a system in use, some files need to be cleaned up or zeroed out after the Flash archive is installed. Examples of these types of files include log files, such as those found in /var/adm and any files in the /var/tmp directory. Log files can be easily zeroed out from a finish script after installation. In the case of temporary directories, such as the /var/tmp directory, it is recommended that they be excluded when the Flash archive is created.

The Flash archive should be created after all software has been installed but before the system has gone into production. And, depending on the software installed and the intended use for the system, the Flash archive may need to be created after the software is installed but before the software has been configured. For example, a database server or LDAP server should have its archive created after the database management software has been installed but before the databases have been created and populated.

Note – An initial installation must be done when a Flash installation is performed. Flash cannot be used to upgrade a system.

Installation of the Solaris OE with a Flash archive can be dramatically faster than with other mechanisms, depending on factors such as network traffic and disk speeds.

Identifying the Master Machine

Before a Flash installation can be performed, a master machine must be identified. The master machine is the system that serves as the template to be copied onto the installation clients. All software and files on the master machine, unless specifically excluded, become a part of the Flash archive and are installed on the client.

Usually, the master machine is not the JumpStart server. However, the JumpStart server is an ideal system to act as a repository for Flash archives. The recommended /jumpstart directory hierarchy used throughout this book should have a /jumpstart/FlashArchives directory added, and the Flash archives should be placed in that directory.

Each system type in your datacenter should have a corresponding archive created to install additional systems of that type. For example, identify an archetypal database server, web server, backup server, etc., and then create Flash archives of those systems to use when new systems need to be deployed.

Store Flash archives offsite, on tape, or on CD-ROM, to prepare for business continuity in the event of a disaster. You can then use these Flash archives at a remote site or disaster recovery site to rapidly deploy software-identical, but not necessarily hardware-identical, replacement systems. See Chapter 11, "System Cloning," for details and procedures of the tape deployment of Flash archives and system cloning.

Creating and Administering Archives

The following flarcreate command creates an archive, named S8-web.archive, of a Solaris 8 4/01 production web server (excluding the /var/tmp directory) with an archive creator string of "j.s.howard@Sun.COM":

```
www06# pwd
/var/tmp/FlashArchives
www06# flarcreate -n "Solaris 8 web server image" \
> -a "j.s.howard@Sun.COM" \
> -R / \
> -x /var/tmp \
> /var/tmp/FlashArchives/S8-web.archive
Determining which filesystems will be included in the archive...
Determining the size of the archive...
The archive will be approximately 446.45MB.
Creating the archive...
Archive creation complete.
```

The -R option specifies to recursively descend from the specified directory, and the -x option excludes the specified directory. See the flarcreate(1M) man page for details on these and other options.

Flash archives can be accessed through NFS or HTTP. Additionally, Flash archives can be written to disk, CD, or tape and subsequently accessed during installation from the disk, CD-ROM, or tape drive local to the client.

Flash archives can be compressed with the -c option to the flarcreate command. Compressed archives are automatically uncompressed before installation after being transferred to the installation client. See the flarcreate(1M) man page for additional details.

Use the flar command to extract information from a specified archive, for example, to determine how an archive was created:

```
www06# flar -i S8-web.archive
archive_id=04291958b038020b87b749ee62085654
files_archived_method=cpio
creation_date=20010326223306
creation_master=www06
content_name=Solaris 8 workgroup server image
files_compressed_method=none
files_archived_size=468105216
content_author=j.s.howard@Sun.COM
content_architecture=sun4u
```

The flar command also provides options to split or combine archives. Consult the flar(1M) man page for additional details on archive usage.

Additional Profile Keywords

Installation of Flash archives is supported by addition of flash_install as a valid value for the installation_type keyword.

Note – Specifying a Flash installation type restricts the number of keywords that can be specified in the profile. See the "Adding the Installation Client" on page 159 for specific details.

The archive_location profile keyword has also been added. The archive_location profile keyword specifies the retrieval method and location, specific to the retrieval method, of the archive:

```
archive_location retrieval_type location_specifier
```

where *retrieval_type* can be any one of the following:
- nfs
- http
- local_tape
- local_device
- local_file

These retrieval types and the location specifier are explained in the following several sections.

Remote Archive Location Specifiers

The nfs and http retrieval types specify the location of the Flash archive on a JumpStart server, NFS server, or HTTP (Web) server. This specification must be provided in one of the following, syntactically equivalent, ways:

> *archive_location* nfs *server*:*/fully/qualified/path/filename*

or:

> *archive_location* nfs://*server*/*fully/qualified/path/filename*

Where:

server is the name of the JumpStart server or the NFS server.

The archive must be shared from the NFS server with options that enable the path to be readable by the client. Additionally, the permissions on the archive file must be such that the file can be read by the client.

The http retrieval type uses the following syntax:

> *archive_location* http *server*:*port_number* */URL/to/file* opts

Where:
- *server* is the HTTP server name.
- *port_number* is the optional port number that the HTTP daemon is listening on (defaults to port 80).
- */full/path/filename* is the fully qualified path to the Flash archive file.
- *opts* are the optional keywords
  - auth basic *username password* specifies the user name and password to access a password-protected HTTP server.

Note – When the user name and password are stored in the JumpStart software profile, they may be readable by *all* users on the system. The use of this option may be a security risk. Therefore, the use of the `auth basic` option is *not* recommended.

- `timeout` *minutes* specifies in minutes the HTTP server timeout value.

- *proxy host:port* specifies the HTTP proxy server and port number.

As with the `nfs` retrieval type, specify the `http` retrieval type in the alternate syntax of:

---

archive_location `http://`*server/URL/to/file* *opts*

Local Archive Location Specifiers

Access the Flash archive from a device local to the installation client. Valid local devices are disk, CD-ROM, or tape devices. To specify a disk device, use the following location specifier:

---

archive_location *local_device* `cXtYdZsN` */full/path/filename* *FStype*

Where:

- `cXtYdZsN` is the Solaris OE device specification for the disk device.

- *FStype* is the optional filesystem type, either `ufs` or `hsfs`. If a filesystem type is not specified, the filesystem is first accessed as `ufs`. If that fails, `hsfs` access is then attempted.

Specify a local tape device as follows:

---

archive_location *local_tape* *tapedevice* *optional_position*

Where:

- *tapedevice* is the full specification to the tape device, for example, `/dev/rmt/0h`.

- *optional_position* is the optional position, specifying the number of End Of File (EOF) marks to skip over on the tape.

Additionally, access archive files from the miniroot by using the `local_file` retrieval type:

---

archive_location   local_file   /full/path/filename

Using Flash in an Example

This section details a complete example of a Flash installation. The major steps of this procedure are these:

1. Identify the master machine and create the Flash archive.

2. Add the installation client (if necessary) on the JumpStart server and edit the appropriate `sysidcfg`, profile, and `rules` files.

3. Initiate the installation on the client.

Creating the Flash Archive

We create the Flash archive on www01, an Ultra Enterprise 220R server acting as a Web server, and then make it available to the JumpStart server, server01, by the `ftp` command.

```
www01# pwd
/var/tmp
www01# uname -a
SunOS www01 5.8 Generic_108528-07 sun4u sparc SUNW,Ultra-60
www01# flarcreate -n "Solaris 8 web server image" \
> -a "j.s.howard@Sun.COM" \
> -R / \
> -x /var/tmp \
> /var/tmp/S8-webserver.archive
Determining which filesystems will be included in the archive...
Determining the size of the archive...
The archive will be approximately 699.92MB.
Creating the archive...
Archive creation complete.
www01# ftp server01
Connected to server01.EE_Lab.Sun.COM.
220 server01 FTP server (SunOS 5.8) ready.
Name (server01:root): blueprints
331 Password required for blueprints.
Password:
230 User blueprints logged in.
ftp> cd /jumpstart/FlashArchives
250 CWD command successful.
ftp> bin
200 Type set to I.
ftp> put S8-webserver.archive
200 PORT command successful.
150 Binary data connection for S8-webserver.archive
(10.1.1.8,34653).
226 Transfer complete.
local: S8-webserver.archive remote: S8-webserver.archive
733880662 bytes sent in 67 seconds (10738.38 Kbytes/s)
ftp> quit
221 Goodbye.
```

Adding the Installation Client

We add the installation client, www26 (a Netra™ t1 105 server) in this example, as an installation client on the JumpStart server, server01 (www26 has already been added to the /etc/ethers and /etc/hosts files).

```
server01# cd /jumpstart/OS/Solaris_8_2001-04/Solaris_8/Tools
server01# ./add_install_client \
> -p server01:/jumpstart/Sysidcfg/Solaris_8 \
> -c server01:/jumpstart \
> www26 sun4u
updating /etc/bootparams
```

The profile used for this example, S8-webserver-Flash.profile, is similar to profiles presented in previous chapters. However, with Flash, only the following profile keywords are valid:

- install_type
- partitioning, and only the keyword values of explicit or existing must be used
- filesys, and the keyword value of auto must *not* be used
- fdisk (valid for Intel Architecture only)

The following profile specifies that Flash is used as the installation type, flash_install. Additionally, the profile instructs that the Flash archive is accessed through NFS, from the location specified by the archive_location keyword.

```
install_type     flash_install
archive_location
nfs://10.1.1.8/jumpstart/FlashArchives/S8-webserver.archive
partitioning     explicit
#
# 4GB / and 1GB swap on a 18GB disk
#
filesys          rootdisk.s0      free           /
filesys          rootdisk.s1      1:449          swap
```

Note – Since name_service=NONE is specified in the following sysidcfg file, an IP address is used for the archive_location in the profile.

The `rules` entry used for this example is as follows:

```
model SUNW,UltraSPARC-IIi-cEngine \
        - \
        Profiles/S8-webserver-Flash.profile \
        Finish/EE_Lab-Flash.fin
```

The `sysidcfg` file used is as follows:

```
system_locale=en_US
timezone=US/Pacific
network_interface=primary {netmask=255.255.255.0
                          protocol_ipv6=no}
terminal=vt100
security_policy=NONE
root_password=QH311oG13nnTU
name_service=NONE
timeserver=localhost
```

Note – A root password is specified in the `sysidcfg` file. This specification overrides the root password contained within the Flash archive in `/etc/shadow`.

After we have created or edited the preceding files, we verify the `rules` file, being certain to use the `check` script from the Solaris 8 OE 4/01 (Update 4) CD-ROM.

```
server01# cd /jumpstart
server01# ./check
Validating rules...
Validating profile Profiles/S8-webserver-Flash.profile...
The custom JumpStart configuration is ok.
```

The finish script used for this installation is:

```
#!/bin/sh
# EE_Lab-Flash.fin
# Finish script for default EE_Lab setup, JumpStart Flash

#
# clean up after flash archive install
#
for i in /a/var/adm/messages* /a/var/adm/utmpx \
        /a/var/adm/wtmpx /a/var/adm/lastlog
do
    cp /dev/null ${i}
done
mkdir /a/var/tmp
chown root:sys /a/var/tmp
chmod 1777 /a/var/tmp
```

Note – The /var/tmp directory needs to be created by the finish script because it was excluded when the archive was created with the flarcreate command.

The boot net - install command is then issued on the installation client.

```
ok boot net - install
Resetting ...

screen not found.
keyboard not found.
Keyboard not present.  Using ttya for input and output.

Netra t1 (UltraSPARC-IIi 360MHz), No Keyboard
OpenBoot 3.10.24 ME, 512 MB memory installed, Serial #11699811.
Ethernet address 8:0:20:b2:86:63, Host ID: 80b28663.

Executing last command: boot net - install
Boot device: /pci@1f,0/pci@1,1/network@1,1  File and args: -
install
SunOS Release 5.8 Version Generic_108528-07 64-bit
Copyright 1983-2001 Sun Microsystems, Inc.  All rights reserved.
whoami: no domain name
Configuring /dev and /devices
Using RPC Bootparams for network configuration information.
Configured interface hme0
Using sysid configuration file
10.1.1.8:/jumpstart/Sysidcfg/Solaris_8/sysidcfg
The system is coming up.  Please wait.
Starting remote procedure call (RPC) services: sysidns done.
Starting Solaris installation program...
Searching for JumpStart directory...
Using rules.ok from 10.1.1.8:/jumpstart.
Checking rules.ok file...
Using profile: Profiles/S8-webserver-Flash.profile
Using finish script: Finish/EE_Lab.fin
Executing JumpStart preinstall phase...
Searching for SolStart directory...
Checking rules.ok file...
Using begin script: install_begin
Using finish script: patch_finish
Executing SolStart preinstall phase...
Executing begin script "install_begin"...
Begin script install_begin execution completed.

Processing default locales
    - Specifying default locale (en_US)

Processing profile
    - Opening Flash archive
```
(continued on next page)

```
(continued from the previous page)
      - Validating Flash archive

      - Selecting all disks
      - Configuring boot device
      - Using disk (c0t0d0) for "rootdisk"
      - Configuring / (c0t0d0s0)
      - Configuring swap (c0t0d0s1)


Verifying space allocation
     NOTE: 1 archives did not include size information


Preparing system for Flash install


Configuring disk (c0t0d0)
      - Creating Solaris disk label (VTOC)


Creating and checking UFS filesystems
      - Creating / (c0t0d0s0)


Beginning Flash archive extraction


Extracting archive: Solaris 8 workgroup server image
      Extracted    0.00 MB (  0% of  699.88 MB archive)
      Extracted    1.00 MB (  0% of  699.88 MB archive)
      Extracted    2.00 MB (  0% of  699.88 MB archive)
                         .
                         .
                output deleted for brevity
                         .
                         .
      Extracted  698.00 MB ( 99% of  699.88 MB archive)
      Extracted  699.00 MB ( 99% of  699.88 MB archive)
      Extracted  699.88 MB (100% of  699.88 MB archive)
      Extraction complete


Customizing system files
      - Mount points table (/etc/vfstab)
      - Network host addresses (/etc/hosts)
(continued on next page)
```

```
(continued from the previous page)
Cleaning devices

Customizing system devices
     - Physical devices (/devices)
     - Logical devices (/dev)

Installing boot information
     - Installing boot blocks (c0t0d0s0)

Installation log location
     - /a/var/sadm/system/logs/install_log (before reboot)
     - /var/sadm/system/logs/install_log (after reboot)

Flash installation complete
Executing JumpStart postinstall phase...
Executing finish script "Finish/EE_Lab-Flash.fin"...


Finish script Finish/EE_Lab-Flash.fin execution completed.

The begin script log 'begin.log'
is located in /var/sadm/system/logs after reboot.

The finish script log 'finish.log'
is located in /var/sadm/system/logs after reboot.
```

Just as with a "classic" JumpStart software installation, *after* the Flash installation completes, the specified finish script executes. If we had specified a begin script, it would have executed *before* the installation began. The Flash mechanism *does not* change the JumpStart framework, but Flash *does* change the manner in which the Solaris OE (and software) is installed. Flash does *not* do an individual installation of each software package, as suninstall does. The Flash mechanism simply writes the archive on the disk and then customizes the on-disk image to the hardware it was just installed on.

Also, keep in mind that the Flash archive is literally a snapshot of an installed system. If the archive was created on a system that has been in production or use, there may be additional clean-up that the finish scripts need to perform. Temporary files such as those found in /var/tmp and log files such as /var/adm/messages, /var/adm/utmpx, and /var/adm/wtmpx should be removed or zeroed out (as appropriate) after a Flash installation from an archive created on a production system. In this example, these files were zeroed out by the finish script.

Summary

This chapter introduced the WebStart Flash facility, available with Solaris 8 OE 4/01 (Update 4). A Flash overview presented the concepts of a Flash archive and recommended appropriate creation times for such an archive.

The chapter described a master machine, recommended a directory hierarchy for the master machine, and suggested storage strategies. The value of Flash archives for business continuity was also noted.

This chapter next demonstrated the use of the `flarcreate` command to create Flash archives and the `flar` command to administer Flash archives. Additionally, the changes to the JumpStart software profile necessary to support Flash installations were described. Those changes include the ability to use `nfs`, `http`, or devices local to the installation client as locations of the Flash archive during installation.

Finally, the chapter illustrated a complete example of creating a Flash archive and installing a Web server with Flash.

## CHAPTER 9

Customizing JumpStart Framework for Installation and Recovery

The JumpStart system is useful for much more than installing the Solaris OE. This chapter examines the more powerful, yet often overlooked, aspects of the JumpStart system. In several ways, the JumpStart system is like a scripting language, the JumpStart framework provides a toolkit of operators that can be used individually or combined. These operators function well individually, but their true power is realized when they are combined.

Note – This chapter provides techniques that can produce configurations that would not be supported by Sun Enterprise Services. However, that lack of support should not detract from the value of the techniques presented.

This chapter examines the boot and installation processes, demonstrating how to adapt these processes for custom system installation and system recovery. This chapter discusses the following topics:

- Building and testing a bootable installation CD-ROM
- Recovering a failed system with JumpStart
- Altering the boot process
- Adding utilities and manual pages
- Meeting challenges unique to the miniroot

Building a Bootable Installation from CD-ROM

There may be some situations when it is not possible to use a JumpStart server, yet it is necessary to perform an automated (hands-free) installation of the Solaris OE. This section details a procedure to create a bootable installation CD-ROM, which is essentially putting a JumpStart server onto a CD. This CD can then be used to effect a standardized, automated Solaris OE installation from the CD. This technique is especially useful in environments where disk space limitations or networking constraints do not allow for a JumpStart server.

This section examines the structure of a bootable Solaris 8 OE (for a SPARC machine) CD and discusses the appropriate modifications to the default installation scripts that allow a JumpStart installation to be done from CD. Further, this section describes how to create a bootable Solaris 8 OE installation CD for the SPARC platform. Additionally, a Solaris 8 OE system with the CD Read/Write (CDRW) utilities installed is used to write the Solaris 8 OE bootable installation CD. Although several different approaches and software applications are available for writing CDs, this section uses commands available only in the standard Solaris 8 OE to write the bootable installation CD.

The structure of the bootable installation CD can vary with different versions of the Solaris OE, partly because of changes required for the support of additional hardware architectures. Additionally, changes to the Solaris OE from version to version may necessitate changes in the CD or the number of CDs required to install the Solaris OE.

Versions of the Solaris OE can vary structurally, but the concepts and procedures presented here can be adapted or extended to create a bootable installation CD for any of the current versions of the Solaris OE.

Bootable CD Structure

A bootable Solaris OE CD has several components in common with any other hard disk. The boot CD is divided into several partitions (or slices), and a Volume Table Of Contents (VTOC) provides the location and sizes of these slices. In addition to the VTOC, a typical installation CD has six slices. Although the Solaris OE imposes the partitioning of the CD into six slices, it is important to note that the CD is written as one *session*—this fact is important when the CD is written.

Following is an examination of the VTOC and the six slices of the Solaris 8 OE installation CD.

Volume Table of Contents

The VTOC is located at cylinder 0, sector 0 on the CD. You can examine the VTOC of any disk device with the `prtvtoc` command. The VTOC of the Solaris 8 OE Software CD (the installation CD) is as follows:

```
server01# /etc/init.d/volmgt stop
server01# prtvtoc /dev/dsk/c0t6d0s0
* /dev/dsk/c0t6d0s0 partition map
*
* Dimensions:
*     512 bytes/sector
*     640 sectors/track
*       1 tracks/cylinder
*     640 sectors/cylinder
*    2048 cylinders
*    2048 accessible cylinders
*
* Flags:
*   1: unmountable
*  10: read-only
*
* Unallocated space:
*       First     Sector    Last
*       Sector    Count     Sector
*       1301760   2560      1304319
*
*                           First     Sector    Last
* Partition  Tag  Flags     Sector    Count     Sector  Mount Directory
           0    4   10            0    1128960   1128959
           1    2   10      1128960     172800   1301759
           2    0   00      1301760       2560   1304319
           3    0   00      1304320       2560   1306879
           4    0   00      1306880       2560   1309439
           5    0   00      1309440       2560   1311999
server01# /etc/init.d/volmgt start
```

Note – You must stop the CD and diskette volume management in order to execute the `prtvtoc` command on a CD. Restart volume management after executing `prtvtoc`. All filesystems mounted from the CD will be unmounted and become inaccessible while volume management is stopped.

In contrast to a hard disk, the disk geometry that the Solaris OE uses for a CD provides no distinction between a cylinder and a track. As the `prtvtoc` output illustrates, the disk label used for a CD defines a cylinder as being composed of one track. Further, the `prtvtoc` output verifies that each track is defined as having 640 sectors and that one sector is equal to 512 bytes.

Note that the Solaris OE requires that all UFS filesystems align on a cylinder boundary. For a CD, this means that all UFS filesystems on the CD must begin on a sector that is a multiple of 640.

Slices

By reading the VTOC, the Solaris OE sees the CD as having six slices. The contents of those six slices are as follows:

- Slice 0 contains the Solaris OE packages to be installed and is the High Sierra File System (HSFS) partition of the CD.
- Slice 1 contains the generic kernel and the directory that becomes the system's / (root) directory after boot.
- Slice 2 contains the boot block for the sun4c architecture.
- Slice 3 contains the boot block for the sun4m architecture.
- Slice 4 contains the boot block for the sun4d architecture.
- Slice 5 contains the boot block for the sun4u architecture.

Slices 2 through 5 are there only to provide hardware-architecture-specific boot blocks. As new hardware architectures are added and old architectures reach their end-of-life, the uses of these slices may change. The file `.slicemapfile` in the top-level directory of slice 0 contains the mapping of a slice to the architecture supported.

As noted earlier, slice 0 is on the HSFS partition and all other slices are on the UFS partitions. Slice 0 is also the largest of the slices and can incorporate any unused space on the CD. The procedures detailed in this section augment the installation procedures in slice 0. However, there is a fixed upper limit in available space for slice 0 that limits our modifications. The total space available on a standard CD is 640 Mbytes. The distribution media for Solaris 8 OE supports four architectures. If the bootable installation CD being created needs to support only one architecture, the space (slices) used by the unneeded architectures can be incorporated into slice 0, enlarging slice 0 but losing the ability to boot other architectures from that CD.

It is also interesting to note that, other than the boot block, the only content of slices 2 through 5 is the file `.SUNW-boot-redirect` in the top-level directory of each of those partitions. This file contains the character 1, which redirects the OpenBoot PROM (OBP) boot loader to load the kernel from partition 1. This mechanism was added with Solaris 2.5 OE as a means of taking advantage of the hardware-independent nature of the kernel to optimize the utilization of space on the CD.

Procedure Overview

Generally, this procedure extracts the contents of slice 0, then splices the desired installation behaviors into the contents of slice 0. The modifications made to slice 0 are to configure the bootable installation CD to partition c0t0d0 as the boot device. The modifications then enable a fully automated installation of the Solaris 8 OE. The profile specifies that a full Solaris OE is installed (the SUNWCall package cluster) with the exception of the Power Management facility.

At a high level, the procedure to create a bootable CD is as follows:

1. Create and populate a work area.

2. Modify the installation behaviors of slice 0.

3. Assemble the individual slices into one CD session and write them to the bootable installation CD.

4. Test the bootable installation CD.

You can also use this procedure to create a bootable CD without the JumpStart software installation behaviors by omitting step 2.

Procedure Specifics

For this example, server01 is an Ultra Enterprise 420R server running the Solaris 8 OE with the Solaris 8 OE CD creation utilities installed and configured as a JumpStart server. server01 has a CD-ROM writer connected at c3t2d0 (identified as cdrom1 by the cdrw -l command).

Creating and Populating a Work Area

Verify the presence of the Solaris OE CD creation utilities. The Solaris 8 OE installation media is already mounted, and /bicd8 is used as the work area. /bicd8 is a 2-Gbyte UFS filesystem.

1. **Create** `/bicd8` **in the following manner:**

```
server01# pkginfo SUNWmkcd SUNWcdrw
system        SUNWcdrw        CD read and write utility for Solaris
system        SUNWmkcd        CD creation utilities
server01# newfs -m 1 /dev/rdsk/c0t1d0s0
newfs: construct a new filesystem /dev/rdsk/c0t1d0s0: (y/n)? y
/dev/rdsk/c0t1d0s0: 4194828 sectors in 1452 cylinders of 27
tracks, 107 sectors
        2048.3MB in 46 cyl groups (32 c/g, 45.14MB/g, 7488 i/g)
super-block backups (for fsck -F ufs -o b=#) at:
 32, 92592, 185152, 277712, 370272, 462832, 555392, 647952, 740512,
833072, 925632, 1018192, 1110752, 1203312, 1295872, 1388432,
1480992, 1573552, 1666112, 1758672, 1851232, 1943792, 2036352,
2128912, 2221472, 2314032, 2406592, 2499152, 2591712, 2684272,
2776832, 2869392, 2958368, 3050928, 3143488, 3236048, 3328608,
3421168, 3513728, 3606288, 3698848, 3791408, 3883968, 3976528,
4069088, 4161648,
server01# mkdir /bicd8
server01# mount /dev/dsk/c0t1d0s0 /bicd8
```

2. **Populate the work area by extracting the partitions from the Solaris 8 OE software CD.**

   a. Since the contents of slice 0 will be manipulated, use `cpio` to copy out partition 0.

   b. Since no changes are made to the contents of slices 1 through 5, use `dd` to take those slices *off* the CD.

   c. Before extracting slices 1 through 5, stop CD and diskette volume management.

   Note – All filesystems mounted from the CD will be unmounted while volume management is stopped.

```
server01# cd /cdrom/sol_8_401_sparc/s0
server01# mkdir /bicd8/s0
server01# find . -print |cpio -pudm /bicd8/s0
server01# cd /bicd8
server01# /etc/init.d/volmgt stop
server01# for i in 1 2 3 4 5
> do
> dd if=/dev/dsk/c0t6d0s${i} of=sol8.s${i} bs=512
> done
172800+0 records in
172800+0 records out
2560+0 records in
2560+0 records out
2560+0 records in
2560+0 records out
2560+0 records in
2560+0 records out
2560+0 records in
2560+0 records out
```

Additionally, since the slice layout of the bootable installation CD being created will not vary from the slice layout of the Solaris 8 OE Software CD, the VTOC from the Software CD can be used later for the bootable installation CD.

3. **Use dd to take the VTOC from the CD, and at this point, restart volume management.**

```
server01# dd if=/dev/dsk/c0t6d0s0 of=/bicd8/sol8.cdrom.vtoc \
> bs=512 count=1
1+0 records in
1+0 records out
server01# /etc/init.d/volmgt start
```

Several choices are available if the slice layout of the CD being created needs to vary from that of the Software CD (for example, if the VTOC needs to be changed). Use CD creation software—such as the toolkit for building bootable CDs, available from Sun Professional Services, Gear Pro for UNIX, or Young Minds—to generate a correct and valid VTOC. Or create a new VTOC and disk label programmatically by creating and writing the dkl_vtoc and dk_label structures, respectively. See the Solaris system file /usr/include/sys/dklabel.h for more information on these structures.

Modifying Installation Behaviors of Slice 0

Modify the default installation behaviors in slice 0 by deleting the contents of the
.install_config directory and adding the desired JumpStart rules and profile to
this directory. Note that the parsed rules.ok file (the output from the check
script), not the rules file, must be placed in the .install_config directory. If any
begin or finish scripts are being used, place them in the .install_config
directory as well.

1. Modify slice 0 as follows.

```
server01# cd /jumpstart
server01# rm /bicd8/s0/.install_config/*
server01# cat /jumpstart/Profiles/S8-Server.profile
install_type      initial_install
system_type       standalone
partitioning      explicit
root_device       c0t0d0s0
#
# 1.5GB / and 512MB swap on a 2GB disk
#
filesys           rootdisk.s0      691:2040         /
filesys           rootdisk.s1      1:690            swap
cluster           SUNWCall
package           SUNWpmowm        delete
package           SUNWpmowr        delete
package           SUNWpmowu        delete
package           SUNWpmr          delete
package           SUNWpmu          delete
package           SUNWpmux         delete
server01# cp /jumpstart/Profiles/S8-server.profile \
> /bicd8/s0/.install_config
server01# cat rules
any - - S8-server.profile -
server01# ./check
Validating rules...
Validating profile S8-server.profile...
The custom JumpStart configuration is ok.
server01# cp rules.ok /bicd8/s0/.install_config
```

The setup of the installation profile directory is controlled by the profind script.
You must modify this script to redirect the configuration directory environment
variable (${SI_CONFIG_DIR}) used by the JumpStart software to the
.install_config directory on the bootable installation CD.

2. **Edit the** `bicd8/s0/Solaris_8/Tools/Boot/usr/sbin/install.d/profind`
shell script and replace the `cdrom()` **function with the following function:**

```
cdrom()
{
    #
    # stub images, indicated by the file /tmp/.preinstall
    #
    if [ -f /tmp/.preinstall ]; then
        mount -o ro -F lofs ${CD_CONFIG_DIR} ${SI_CONFIG_DIR}
>/dev/null 2>&1

        if [ $? -eq 0 ]; then
            verify_config "defaults" "CDROM"
        fi
    fi
    gettext " <<< using CD default >>>"; echo      # added bicd8
    rmdir ${SI_CONFIG_DIR}                          # added bicd8
    ln -s /cdrom/.install_config ${SI_CONFIG_DIR}  # added bicd8
    exit 0                                          # added bicd8
}
```

This modification instructs the installation process to use the `.install_config` directory that was populated with the desired JumpStart software profiles and `rules` file.

Assembling and Writing Slices to Bootable Installation CD

At this point, the VTOC, the modified slice 0, and the unmodified slices 1 through 5 are written to the bootable installation CD being created. The individual slices are combined into one image to be written to a blank CD.

It is important to keep in mind that slice 0 of the Solaris 8 OE CD is at almost 100 percent utilization of the total available space of slice 0. Further, the Solaris 8 OE product is on two CDs because all of the software package will not fit on one CD. If the modified slice 0 exceeds the size of the original slice 0, you must either create a new VTOC or remove unneeded files from slice 0. Also keep in mind that the iso9660 filesystem has some overhead, which increases the image (created by `mkisofs`) as well.

1. **Create an automated install CD (without having to swap CDs during the installation), by removing from slice 0 those software packages that will not be installed or are not needed by the installation client.**

Additionally, removing unneeded files from slice 0 is much simpler than handcrafting a VTOC. A good place to start removing unneeded files is the `Product` subdirectory. Rarely does a Solaris OE installation require all the packages from the `Product` directory. For example, most servers do not (and should not) have the power management packages installed. Removing the power management packages before executing the `mkisofs` command helps minimize the size of the created iso9660 HSFS image.

Remember that the profile you are using should reflect these changes to the `Product` directory; that is, don't try to install the removed packages. The removed packages should also be removed from the software package cluster definition file, `/bicd8/s0/Solaris_8/Product/.clustertoc`.

2. **Before combining and writing the CD, execute the** `mkisofs` **command to convert the modified slice 0 in the** `/bicd8/s0` **work area into an HSFS filesystem.**

3. **Since no changes to the miniroot or supported architectures are required, extract slices 1 through 5 from the Solaris 8 OE software CD and write them, unchanged, to the bootable installation CD being created.**

4. It is important to note that `mkisofs` creates a VTOC at offset 0 within this image.

   Use dd to remove this invalid VTOC from the HSFS image by skipping the first 512-byte block. For this example, the unneeded power management packages are removed from the `Product` directory before the iso9660 filesystem is created from `/bicd/s0`.

```
server01# cd /bicd8/s0/Solaris_8/Product
server01# rm -rf SUNWpmowr/* SUNWpmowu/* SUNWpmr/* SUNWpmux/*
server01# cd /bicd8
server01# mkisofs -R -d -L -l -o /bicd8/sol8.S0 /bicd8/s0
        .
        .
        .

Total extents actually written = 282170
Total translation table size: 0
Total rockridge attributes bytes: 4246465
Total directory bytes: 24463360
Path table size(bytes): 175770
Max brk space used 167a000
282170 extents written (551 Mb)
server01# dd if=/bicd8/sol8.S0 of=/bicd8/new.sol8.s0 bs=512 skip=1
1128679+0 records in
1128679+0 records out
server01# rm /bicd8/sol8.S0
```

5. The VTOC specifies a size for slice 0, so slice 0 must be padded to maintain the validity of the VTOC and maintain the correct cylinder boundaries. The size of the pad is computed by adding 1 to the number of sectors in the HSFS slice 0 image (this accounts for the VTOC) then subtracting that sum from the number of sectors (reported by prtvtoc) in the unmodified slice 0 on the CD.

Create the pad by using dd **to read the appropriate number of zeros from** /dev/zero.

```
server01# bc
1128960-(1128679+1)
280
server01# dd if=/dev/zero of=pad.s0 bs=512 count=280
280+0 records in
280+0 records out
```

6. As with any automated installation, sysidtool needs all installation client identification information such as host name, IP address, time zone, etc. The location of this information depends on whether the installation client is connected to a network or off-network during the installation. If the installation client is connected to a network during installation, this information must be available from a name service such as NIS+ or NIS, or provided from the /etc/bootparams, /etc/ethers, and sysidcfg files from a host on the network. The minimum entries required in the /etc/bootparams file are as follows:

```
server01# cat /etc/bootparams
client06 sysid_config=server01:/jumpstart/Sysidcfg/Solaris_8
```

The sysidcfg file specified by /etc/bootparams contains the following:

```
server01# cat /jumpstart/Sysidcfg/Solaris_8/sysidcfg
system_locale=en_US
timezone=US/Pacific
network_interface=primary   {netmask=255.255.255.0
                            protocol_ipv6=no}
terminal=vt100
security_policy=NONE
root_password=Q7jsh1m6IztTU
name_service=NONE
timeserver=localhost
```

To perform an automated installation without network connectivity, you must have placed a `sysidcfg` file in the `/etc` directory of the filesystem image taken from slice 1 of the Solaris 8 OE CD.

Mount the filesystem image file by using the Solaris 8 OE loopback file driver administration commands.

7. **After mounting the filesystem image, use standard Solaris OE commands to remove the symbolic link for the default `sysidcfg` file and to copy a complete `sysidcfg` file to the filesystem image.**

```
server01# cat /bicd8/sysidcfg
system_locale=en_US
timezone=US/Pacific
network_interface=primary {hostname=client06
                           ip_address=10.1.1.9
                           netmask=255.255.255.0
                           protocol_ipv6=no}
terminal=vt100
security_policy=NONE
root_password=Q7jsh1m6IztTU
name_service=NONE
timeserver=localhost
server01# lofiadm -a /bicd8/sol8.s1
/dev/lofi/1
server01# mount /dev/lofi/1 /mnt
server01# ls -al /mnt/etc/sysidcfg
lrwxrwxrwx   1 root      other         24 Nov 28 16:38
/mnt/etc/sysidcfg -> ../tmp/root/etc/sysidcfg
server01# rm /mnt/etc/sysidcfg
server01# cp /bicd8/sysidcfg /mnt/etc/sysidcfg
server01# umount /mnt
server01# lofiadm -d /dev/lofi/1
```

Note – For the off-network automated installation, the host name, IP address, netmask, and IPv6 specification *must* be in the `sysidcfg` file.

See Chapter 11, "System Cloning," for a fully automated technique for a JumpStart software installation with no network connectivity, using the WebStart Flash extensions.

8. **Concatenate the VTOC, HSFS image, padding, and unmodified images of slices 1 through 5 into one image and write it to the CD writer on device** `c3t2d0` **with the** cdrw **command:**

```
server01# cat sol8.cdrom.vtoc new.sol8.s0 pad.s0 \
sol8.s1 sol8.s2 sol8.s3 sol8.s4 sol8.s5 >bicd8.image
server01# cdrw -d cdrom1 -i bicd8.image
Initializing device...done.
Writing track 1...done.
done.
Finalizing (Can take up to 4 minutes)...done.
```

Testing the Bootable Installation CD

To validate the newly created bootable installation CD, place it in the CD drive of the installation client, client06. For this example, the client is off-network while the installation occurs and the sysidcfg file in the /etc directory of slice 1 of the CD was modified, as shown in step 3 of "Procedure Specifics" on page 171. After the OBP boot cdrom command is issued, client06 boots from the CD and performs an automated installation of the Solaris 8 OE.

Issue the boot cdrom command with the - install options to initiate the automated installation:

```
screen not found.
{0} ok boot cdrom - install
Boot device: /pci@1f,4000/scsi@3/disk@6,0:f  File and args: -
install

SunOS Release 5.8 Version Generic_108528-05 64-bit
Copyright 1983-2000 Sun Microsystems, Inc.  All rights reserved.
Configuring /dev and /devices
Using RPC Bootparams for network configuration information.
SUNW,hme0 : No response from Ethernet network : Link down -- cable
problem?
Skipping interface hme0
SUNW,hme0 : No response from Ethernet network : Link down -- cable
problem?

The system is coming up.  Please wait.
SUNW,hme0 : No response from Ethernet network : Link down -- cable
problem?
(continued on next page)
```

```
(continued from previous page)
Starting remote procedure call (RPC) services: sysidns done.
Starting Solaris installation program...
Searching for JumpStart directory...
SUNW,hme0 : No response from Ethernet network : Link down -- cable
problem?
<<< using CD default >>>
Checking rules.ok file...
Using profile: S8-server.profile
Executing JumpStart preinstall phase...
Searching for SolStart directory...
Checking rules.ok file...
Using begin script: install_begin
Using finish script: patch_finish
Executing SolStart preinstall phase...
Executing begin script "install_begin"...
Begin script install_begin execution completed.

Processing default locales
    - Specifying default locale (en_US)
Processing profile
    - Selecting cluster (SUNWCall)
    - Deselecting package (SUNWpmowm)
    - Deselecting package (SUNWpmowr)
    - Deselecting package (SUNWpmowu)
    - Deselecting package (SUNWpmr)
    - Deselecting package (SUNWpmu)
    - Deselecting package (SUNWpmux)
    - Selecting locale (en_US)

Installing 64 bit Solaris packages
    - Selecting all disks
    - Configuring boot device
    - Using disk (c0t0d0) for "rootdisk"
    - Configuring / (c0t0d0s0)
    - Configuring swap (c0t0d0s1)
    - Deselecting unmodified disk (c0t1d0)
    - Deselecting unmodified disk (c1t8d0)
    - Deselecting unmodified disk (c1t9d0)
    - Deselecting unmodified disk (c1t10d0)
    - Deselecting unmodified disk (c1t11d0)
    - Deselecting unmodified disk (c1t12d0)
    - Deselecting unmodified disk (c1t13d0)
    - Deselecting unmodified disk (c2t0d0)
    - Deselecting unmodified disk (c2t1d0)
(continued on next page)
```

```
(continued from previous page)
    - Deselecting unmodified disk (c2t2d0)
    - Deselecting unmodified disk (c2t3d0)
    - Deselecting unmodified disk (c2t4d0)
    - Deselecting unmodified disk (c2t5d0)

Verifying disk configuration
    - WARNING: Unused disk space (c0t0d0)
    - WARNING: Changing the system's default boot device in the
EEPROM
Verifying space allocation

    - Total software size:  737.00 Mbytes

Preparing system for Solaris install

Configuring disk (c0t0d0)
    - Creating Solaris disk label (VTOC)
Creating and checking UFS filesystems
    - Creating / (c0t0d0s0)

Beginning Solaris software installation
Starting software installation
    SUNWxwrtx...done.  736.96 Mbytes remaining.
    SUNWxwrtl...done.  736.91 Mbytes remaining.
    SUNWwbapi...done.  736.40 Mbytes remaining.
                   .
                   . (package listing deleted for brevity)
                   .

    SUNWnamos...done.  257.17 Mbytes remaining.
    SUNWnamow...done.  257.09 Mbytes remaining.
    SUNWnamox...done.  256.90 Mbytes remaining.

Completed software installation

Customizing system files
    - Mount points table (/etc/vfstab)
    - Unselected disk mount points
(/var/sadm/system/data/vfstab.unselected)
    - Network host addresses (/etc/hosts)

Customizing system devices
    - Physical devices (/devices)
    - Logical devices (/dev)
(continued on next page)
```

```
(continued from previous page)
Installing boot information
    - Installing boot blocks (c0t0d0s0)
    - Updating system firmware for automatic rebooting

Installation log location
    - /a/var/sadm/system/logs/install_log (before reboot)
    - /var/sadm/system/logs/install_log (after reboot)
Installation complete
Executing SolStart postinstall phase...
Executing finish script "patch_finish"...

Finish script patch_finish execution completed.
Executing JumpStart postinstall phase...
The begin script log 'begin.log'
is located in /var/sadm/system/logs after reboot.


The finish script log 'finish.log'
is located in /var/sadm/system/logs after reboot.

syncing filesystems... done
rebooting...
Resetting ...

screen not found.
Can't open input device.
Keyboard not present.  Using ttya for input and output.

Sun Ultra 60 UPA/PCI (2 X UltraSPARC-II 450MHz), No Keyboard
OpenBoot 3.27, 2048 MB memory installed, Serial #13100146.
Ethernet address 8:0:20:c8:ff:fa, Host ID: 80c8fffa.

Initializing Memory
Rebooting with command: boot
Boot device: disk:a  File and args:
SunOS Release 5.8 Version Generic_108528-05 64-bit
Copyright 1983-2000 Sun Microsystems, Inc.  All rights reserved.
configuring IPv4 interfaces: hme0.
Hostname: client06
Configuring /dev and /devices
Configuring the /dev directory (compatibility devices)
The system is coming up.  Please wait.
Configuring network interface addresses: hme0
(continued on next page)
```

```
(continued from previous page)
SUNW,hme0 : No response from Ethernet network : Link down -- cable
problem?
SUNW,hme0 : No response from Ethernet network : Link down -- cable
problem?
  .
SUNW,hme0 : No response from Ethernet network : Link down -- cable
problem?
SUNW,hme0 : No response from Ethernet network : Link down -- cable
problem?
RPC: Timed out
SUNW,hme0 : No response from Ethernet network : Link down -- cable
problem?
SUNW,hme0 : No response from Ethernet network : Link down -- cable
problem?
Starting IPv4 routing daemon.
starting rpc services: rpcbind done.
System identification is completed.
Setting netmask of hme0 to 255.255.255.0
SUNW,hme0 : No response from Ethernet network : Link down -- cable
problem?
Setting default IPv4 interface for multicast: add net 224.0/4:
gateway client06
syslog service starting.
Print services started.
volume management starting.
The system is ready.

client06 console login:
```

Note – The repeated warnings about the lack of network response and the RPC
time-out error during the postinstallation boot are due to the installation client being
disconnected from the network.

Recovering a Failed System with JumpStart

The typical mechanism for attempting recovery on a failed system is to boot the host from the Solaris OE installation CD. This approach is the most direct method to bring the to-be-recovered host to a point where some form of corrective action can be initiated. However, this method does have a major drawback: the unalterable nature of the CD restricts the available tools and thereby restricts the recovery procedures or adversely affects the recovery time. Tools commonly used in the datacenter, such as Veritas Volume Manager (VxVM), Veritas NetBackup, or Solstice Backup™ software are either completely unavailable or very cumbersome to use when booted from the CD.

Booting from the network with JumpStart technology is virtually identical to booting from the CD-ROM. Although the mechanics of access to the filesystem and data files may differ between a network boot and a CD boot, the operating environment image loaded when booting from the network is identical to the one loaded when booting from the CD-ROM. In addition, booting from the network restricts the system administrator in the same fashion as booting from the CD itself; the root filesystem provided to the client is mounted read-only. However, since the JumpStart server's boot image originates on writable media, it can be modified at the server side before the client is booted.

JumpStart Recovery Techniques

An example of this concept is patching the JumpStart boot image for the Solaris OE. The boot image is patched, on the server, with the `patchadd` command. When a client does a network boot, it is served the patched kernel. Similarly to this straightforward patching procedure, the boot image can also be changed to allow a different startup processing or can even be augmented with other tools that might prove useful during a service event or a system recovery.

Additionally, by modifying the client's boot image, you can install software tools commonly used in the datacenter into the JumpStart boot image and configure them for use by any system which uses that boot image.

Further, by installing Solaris for IA on a laptop and modifying the JumpStart miniroot on the laptop, you can create a mobile recovery server. This mobile recovery server can then be deployed onto whatever subnet is necessary at the time of system recovery.

$ROOTDIR Directory

To understand how to correctly modify or augment the client's boot image, you must understand how the JumpStart server maps the filesystem that contains the boot image to the client's view of the same filesystem. For example, to modify the network services available on the client, you may need to modify the client's /etc/inetd.conf file. If this is the case, you must locate and modify the client's /etc/inetd.conf file on the JumpStart server.

This information is controlled, in part, by the manner in which the JumpStart server was installed. /jumpstart is the filesystem that is used as the location for all JumpStart configuration information, profiles, boot images, and software installation packages.

1. **Use commands** setup_install_server **and** add_to_install_server **to copy the boot image and install packages from the Solaris OE Software CD-ROMs to the specified directory (**/jumpstart/OS/Solaris_8_2001-04**) on the JumpStart server.**

2. **Execute the** add_install_client **command to configure the sample client (**client06**) to boot from this server image.**

3. **Use the** add_install_client **command to update (or create if necessary) the**/etc/bootparams **file containing the information for the specified client.**

4. **Specify the** -e **and** -i **options and instruct** add_install_client **to update** /etc/ethers **and** /etc/hosts, **respectively, if necessary.**

   /jumpstart is shared through the NFS system with read-only access rights and the effective UID of unknown users mapped to root. For the anon=0 option, see the share_nfs(1M) man page for additional details.

The following command sample illustrates a typical installation and configuration of a JumpStart server.

```
server01# share -F nfs -o ro,anon=0 /jumpstart
server01# mkdir /jumpstart/OS/Solaris_8_2001-04
server01# cd /cdrom/sol_8_401_sparc/s0/Solaris_8/Tools
server01# ./setup_install_server /jumpstart/OS/Solaris_8_2001-
04
Verifying target directory...
Calculating the required disk space for the Solaris_8 product
Copying the CD image to disk...
Install Server setup complete
[ insert Solaris 8 Software cd 2 of 2 ]
server01# cd /cdrom/sol_8_401_sparc_2/Solaris_8/Tools
server01# ./add_to_install_server /jumpstart/OS/Solaris_8_2001-
04

The following Products will be copied to
/jumpstart/OS/Solaris_8_2001-04/Solaris_8/Product:

Solaris_2_of_2

If only a subset of products is needed enter Control-C
and invoke ./add_to_install_server with the -s option.

Checking required disk space...

Copying the Early Access products...
213481 blocks


Processing completed successfully.
server01# cd /jumpstart/OS/Solaris_8_2001-04/Solaris_8/Tools
server01#./add_install_client \
> -i 129.153.47.6 -e 8:0:20:7c:ff:d0 \
> -p server01:/jumpstart/Sysidcfg/Solaris_8 \
> -c server01:/jumpstart \
> client06 sun4u
```

Examination of `/etc/bootparams` shows how the JumpStart server, `server01`, view of the client's root filesystem is mapped to the client server, `client06`, view.

```
client06  root=server01:/jumpstart/OS/Solaris_8_2001-
04/Solaris_8/Tools/Boot
install=server01:/jumpstart/OS/Solaris_8_2001-04 boottype=:in
sysid_config=server01:/jumpstart/Sysidcfg/Solaris_8
install_config=server01:/jumpstart rootopts=:rsize=32768
```

The parameter `root` is set to `server01:/jumpstart/OS/Solaris_8_2001-04/Solaris_8/Tools/Boot`. This is what the NFS filesystem `client06` mounts as its root filesystem when booting over the network. Since the JumpStart environment variable, `$ROOTDIR`, is set to this value, the JumpStart server's view of this directory is commonly referred to as `$ROOTDIR`. In this example, `$ROOTDIR` is set to `server01:/jumpstart/OS/Solaris_8_2001-04/Solaris_8/Tools/Boot`. Locating or placing a file into the client's filesystem on the JumpStart server simply becomes a matter of prefixing `$ROOTDIR` to the file. For example, if the client needs to have a file placed in its `/etc` directory, that file must be placed in `$ROOTDIR/etc` on the JumpStart server.

Altering the Boot Process

This section demonstrates how to augment the client's boot image to make it suitable for use as a platform for system recovery operations:

- Modify the option and argument processing during boot
- Provide services and daemons
- Provide an interactive shell

It is important to note that the following modifications to the client's boot image offer additional functionality. The default functionality of the client's boot image remains unchanged, and you can still use the client's boot image to install the Solaris OE.

The first challenge in transforming the install boot image into a boot image suitable for recovery operations is to change the boot process, or startup process, of the miniroot. The client should come up to multiuser mode, yet not enter the default action of beginning the installation process. To take control away from the default boot process, you must modify the scripts that run at startup time on the client.

Processing Options and Arguments During Boot

The first task in converting the install boot image into a recovery boot image is to augment the boot process with a "recover" mode. You do that by altering the boot parameter processing logic in the startup scripts. For example, the OBP boot command, `boot net - install`, is normally used to perform a JumpStart (network) boot and installation. The `install` argument is passed through the kernel and to `init` as the system startup scripts are executed. We want to find where that argument is parsed and add logic to allow other keywords (such as `recover`).

The OBP passes options to the kernel, such as the `-s` (boot to single-user mode) and `-r` (initiate a device tree rebuild and kernel reconfiguration) options. In this instance the kernel is `genunix`, the miniroot. The OBP passes arguments along to the kernel as well. Since the kernel does not process command-line arguments (it only processes the options it recognizes), the arguments are ignored by the kernel and passed along to `init`. To prevent confusion, kernel switches and arguments are separated by a lone dash, which is why the space following the minus character (`-`) is crucial in the command `boot net - install`.

In turn, `init` passes all arguments on to the scripts that it calls. FIGURE 9-1 shows an overview of the startup process.

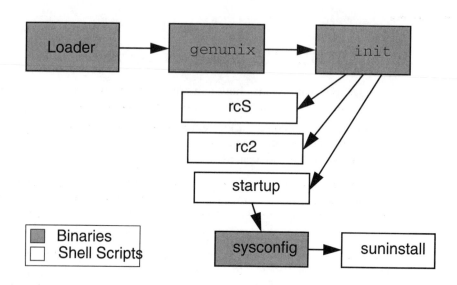

FIGURE 9-1   Overview of the Startup Process

By using the processing control table used by `init`, $ROOTDIR/etc/inittab, as a road map to the startup processing, you can determine that $ROOTDIR/sbin/rcS is where the argument processing takes place. The portion of $ROOTDIR/sbin/rcS relevant to the argument processing is as follows:

```
set -- ""
set -- '/sbin/getbootargs 2>/dev/null'
if [ $# -gt 0 ] ; then
        while [ $# -gt 0 ] ; do
                case $1 in
            FD=*)
# at end of script, save root dev in /tmp/.preinstall
# this is an unambiguous indication of stub boot
                        FJS_BOOT="yes"
                    From='(IFS="="; set -- $1; echo "$2 $3 $4 $5" )'
                        break
                        ;;
                browser)
                        cat < /dev/null > /tmp/.install_boot
                        cat < /dev/null > /tmp/.smi_boot
                        shift
                        ;;

                install)
                        INSTALL_BOOT="yes"
                        cat < /dev/null > /tmp/.install_boot
                        shift
                dhcp)
                        TRY_DHCP="yes"
                        shift
                        ;;
                tape*)
                        echo "$1" >/tmp/.cjfiles_method
                        shift
                        ;;

                mansysid)
                        cat < /dev/null > /tmp/.manual-sysid
                        shift
                        ;;

                w)
                        cat < /dev/null > /tmp/.nowin
                        shift
                        ;;
                *)
                        shift
                        ;;
                esac
        done
fi
```

It is now relatively straightforward to add recognition and processing for the recover argument by adding another "word" to the case statement. The modified section of $ROOTDIR/sbin/rcS is as follows:

```
set -- ""
set -- '/sbin/getbootargs 2>/dev/null'
if [ $# -gt 0 ] ; then
        while [ $# -gt 0 ] ; do
                case $1 in
             FD=*)
# at end of script, save root dev in /tmp/.preinstall
# this is an unambiguous indication of stub boot
                        FJS_BOOT="yes"
                      From='(IFS="="; set -- $1; echo "$2 $3 $4 $5" )'
                        break
                        ;;
                browser)
                        cat < /dev/null > /tmp/.install_boot
                        cat < /dev/null > /tmp/.smi_boot
                        shift
                        ;;
                recover)
                        cat < /dev/null > /tmp/._recover_startup
                        shift
                        ;;
                install)
                        INSTALL_BOOT="yes"
                        cat < /dev/null > /tmp/.install_boot
                        shift
                dhcp)
                        TRY_DHCP="yes"
                        shift
                        ;;
                tape*)
                        echo "$1" >/tmp/.cjfiles_method
                        shift
                        ;;
                mansysid)
                        cat < /dev/null > /tmp/.manual-sysid
                        shift
                        ;;

                w)
                        cat < /dev/null > /tmp/.nowin
                        shift
                        ;;
                *)
                        shift
                        ;;
                esac
        done
fi
```

It is important to note that almost no action is performed within the case statement or $ROOTDIR/sbin/rcS. As in the case of the install argument, the processing of the recover argument consists *only* of creating a state file (or flag file). Using this mechanism eases the decision process in scripts executed later, without the need to parse the arguments directly. If recovery scripts or tools must start automatically on a recovery boot or if scripts must determine the state of the system and take appropriate action, these scripts *only* need to check for the existence of the file /tmp/._recover_startup to determine the system's state. Because this method of modifying $ROOTDIR/sbin/rcS reduces complexity and minimizes the opportunity for human error in modifying the crucial $ROOTDIR/sbin/rcS script, it is strongly recommended that you use the same or a similar approach whenever adding additional startup processing.

Providing Services for Recovery

The default boot process does not start any service daemons that are not required by the Solaris OE installation process. However, some of these daemons may facilitate or are needed during a system recovery operation. For example, the Internet service daemon, inetd, is not needed for installation. However, a recovery operation is greatly facilitated by having inetd start automatically on a recovery boot.

Unfortunately, daemons can be started from many scripts and there is no reference or mapping of where a particular daemon may be started. However, most of the standard or common Solaris OE daemons are present, but commented out (referred to as *stubbed*), in the startup scripts executed by init. The only recourse is to follow the execution flow of the scripts launched by init to locate what services are started from which scripts, uncommenting the required daemons. For example, inetd is present but commented out in $ROOTDIR/sbin/sysconfig. To start inetd during a recovery boot, modify $ROOTDIR/sbin/sysconfig (at the point where inetd startup is commented out), as follows:

```
if [ -f /tmp/._recover_startup ] ; then
    /usr/sbin/inetd -s
fi
```

Starting inetd is sufficient for the most common network services. "Adding a Recovery Tool" on page 192 gives an example of adding additional services. If a service or daemon is required at startup but is not stubbed in one of the startup scripts, you must add the invocation to the startup processing. If it is necessary to add a call to a script or the execution of a command, it is recommended that the addition be done as late as possible in the startup sequence to avoid impacting dependencies or setup work that services may have on other services or daemons. For example, many network services require that sysidnet has been run, which implies the presence of a name service or sysidcfg file.

Providing an Interactive Shell

The default installation boot image enters the installation utility (suninstall) at the end of its startup processing. To have the default installation boot image act as a recovery platform, you will find it advantageous to provide an interactive shell rather than to execute suninstall. To provide the interactive shell, add the following lines to the end of $ROOTDIR/sbin/sysconfig.

```
if [ -f /tmp/._recover_startup ] ; then
    echo "Starting interactive Korn shell..."
    exec /bin/ksh -o vi
fi
```

Adding Utilities and Manual Pages

The methodology of the previous section can also be applied to the task of augmenting the client's boot image with tools, utilities, and documentation. Most of the tools to be added to the client's boot image do not require special configuration. In most cases, the utility or tool only needs to be copied into its expected location under $ROOTDIR to be accessible and usable by the client after a boot net - recover. However, it is important to note that device drivers, kernel extensions, and utilities expecting a writable /var/tmp are a special case that is examined in "Files in /var" on page 195.

Adding a Recovery Tool

Let's take Solstice Backup software as an example of adding a recovery tool to a client's boot image. Solstice Backup software installs its client-side utilities in /usr/bin/nsr and /usr/lib/nsr. To provide the client portions of Solstice Backup software to the client's recovery boot image, you need only replicate or relocate the /usr/bin/nsr and /usr/lib/nsr directory hierarchies on the JumpStart server in $ROOTDIR/usr/bin/nsr and $ROOTDIR/usr/lib/nsr, respectively. You accomplish this relocation by using the root-path option (-R) of pkgadd or simply by copying the directory hierarchies from an installed Solstice Backup Client to $ROOTDIR/usr/bin/nsr and $ROOTDIR/usr/lib/nsr.

Adding Device Drivers

As with system services and daemons, the only device drivers provided in the default client's boot image are those device drivers that may be necessary for installing the Solaris OE. Providing the client's recovery boot image with additional device drivers, such as FDDI, ATM, or some other high-bandwidth network driver, can be useful or required in system recovery situations.

Consider the FDDI network interface. The default client's boot image does not provide this device driver. However, many datacenters use a dedicated FDDI network for backups and restores. During a recovery operation, the system administrator would benefit from having the recovery boot image available to access this high-bandwidth network to recover data from the backup server.

In principle, device drivers are added in much the same way that standard files are added to the JumpStart server. Device drivers or kernel extensions are merely copied to $ROOTDIR/kernel/drv. Unfortunately, a device driver may need to modify several other configuration files in order to function properly. The Solaris add_drv command is the mechanism by which the required files can be updated in a controlled fashion. For example, to add the FDDI driver to the recovery boot image, execute the following commands:

```
server01# ROOTDIR=/jumpstart/OS/Solaris_8_2001-
04/Solaris_8/Tools/Boot ; export ROOTDIR
server01# cd /kernel/drv
server01# cp fddi fddi.conf $ROOTDIR/kernel/drv
server01# add_drv -b $ROOTDIR /kernel/drv/fddi
```

Note – Before installation, consult the manufacturer or vendor instructions for all device drivers.

For most drivers, these commands are sufficient for installation into the recovery boot image. However, some device drivers, such as those that create or require entries in /dev upon boot, may require further configuration by hand. Some device drivers may require modifications to files such as these:

- $ROOTDIR/etc/devlink.tab
- $ROOTDIR/etc/driver_aliases
- $ROOTDIR/etc/system

After you configure the drivers by hand, you must then appropriately modify the respective files under $ROOTDIR in order to affect the client's boot image. Consult the installation documentation for the device driver for any specific modifications that may be necessary.

For example, the Veritas Volume Manager (VxVM) product includes the device drivers vxspec, vxio, and vxdmp. In addition to copying these drivers into $ROOTDIR/kernel/drv, you must load these device drivers at boot by adding the following directives to $ROOTDIR/etc/system.

```
forceload drv/vxdmp
forceload drv/vxspec
forceload drv/vxio
```

Additionally, these VxVM device drivers require device entries to be created in /dev according to the specific template in /etc/devlink.tab.

Meeting Challenges Unique to the Miniroot

As previously discussed, the miniroot is a subset Solaris OE kernel and filesystem. The miniroot must fit in a prescribed amount of physical memory and so does not contain all of the software packages that an installed system would contain. In addition to the size limitations, there are challenges in installation that are unique to the miniroot. This section covers these specific challenges:

- Read-only media
- Files in /var
- path_to_inst file

Read-Only Media

While it is obvious that the boot image on a Solaris OE Software CD is read-only, it may not be obvious that the client's boot image served by the JumpStart server is also read-only. Because of this, all systems booted from this image for recovery or installation mount their filesystems read-only. Whether booted from a CD or over the network from a JumpStart server, the /tmp memory-mapped tmpfs filesystem is the only writable space for any utility or service that requires writable media.

The Solaris OE tmpfs filesystem is fashioned from the virtual memory in the client and as such, it loses all its contents when the client reboots. Any file or directory on the remaining filesystems that must behave as if it is writable must be redirected to /tmp by means of a symbolic link. For example, the /etc/vfstab file must be writable, but /etc is on a read-only filesystem. The file /etc/vfstab is actually a symbolic link, created at the client's boot, to a writable vfstab file in /tmp. All such writable file links are created on the read-only CD image or on the client's boot image on the JumpStart server. The targets of all such symbolic links are then created in /tmp when the miniroot is booted.

The same mechanism can be used to provide writable space for tools added to the recovery boot image. The following commands provide a writable log space for NetBackup in $ROOTDIR/usr/openv/logs.

```
server01# cd /jumpstart/OS/Solaris_8_2001-
04/Solaris_8/Tools/Boot/usr/openv
server01# ln -s /tmp/_openv_logs ./logs
```

However, this approach addresses only half the problem. The target of the symbolic link, in /tmp, must still be populated at boot. Any required link targets in /tmp can be populated by one of the following methods:

1. Create a start script that executes mkdir /tmp/_openv_logs.

2. Utilize the built-in script for populating /tmp.

Method one is a brute force approach, but effective on a small or limited scale. The second method takes advantage of the existing method that the miniroot uses at boot to populate /tmp.

A prototype (or template for) /tmp is maintained on the miniroot and is copied into /tmp very early in the boot cycle. This prototype is the directory $ROOTDIR/.tmp_proto. Early in the startup sequence (in $ROOTDIR/sbin/rcS), cpio is used to populate /tmp from this prototype. These prototypes become the targets referenced by symbolic links throughout the miniroot image.

For our example above, creating the directory $ROOTDIR/.tmp_proto/_openv_logs ensures that /tmp/_openv_logs are created when the client miniroot is started.

Files in /var

The /var directory tree is an extension of the writable directory problem outlined in "Adding Utilities and Manual Pages" on page 192. Most facilities in the Solaris OE utilize /var/tmp or write temporary files into some subdirectory of /var. Because so many utilities expect /var to be writable, the entire /var filesystem is made writable by means of a symbolic link from /var to /tmp/var. This is accomplished by the same mechanism as described in "Adding Utilities and Manual Pages" on page 192. The prototype for the /var hierarchy is in $ROOTDIR/.tmp_proto/var. For a file or directory to be relocated into the client's /var, the file or directory must be the $ROOTDIR/.tmp_proto/var prototype.

`path_to_inst` File

The Solaris OE device instance number file, `path_to_inst`, is a special case. It is special because this file must be created from scratch each time a system boots from the miniroot. The `path_to_inst` file must be writable; however, it cannot simply link to `/tmp`.

The miniroot cannot possibly have a valid device tree and instance number file for each client that might boot from it. The `path_to_inst` file and the `/dev` and `/devices` directory trees must be created by the miniroot each time a system boots from the CD or JumpStart boot image. The OBP is responsible for probing the bus and inventorying all of the devices in the system. The OBP hands off the result of this inventory (the OBP device tree) to the kernel when it begins loading. The OBP device tree is used as the basis for the kernel to map the device location (path) to the device driver instance numbers. This mapping is what is stored in the `path_to_inst` file. For a boot from read-only media (for example, from CD or from a JumpStart server) the newly created `path_to_inst` file is generated and written to `/tmp/root/etc/path_to_inst` early in the miniroot boot process.

Because a valid `/etc/path_to_inst` is required by the kernel very early in the boot cycle, using a writable surrogate in `/tmp` is not possible, since `/tmp` is not yet populated when the instance number file is needed.

For the kernel to be redirected to the *real* `path_to_inst` file that was written in `/tmp/root/etc/path_to_inst`, *two* `path_to_inst` files are used. The *real* `path_to_inst`, which contains valid device paths mapped to the correct instance names, is created in `/tmp/root/etc/path_to_inst`. The bootstrap version, required by the kernel but invalidated after the kernel loads, is in `/etc`. This bootstrap version of `$ROOTDIR/etc/path_to_inst` consists only of the line:

```
#path_to_inst_bootstrap_1
```

This bootstrap `path_to_inst` can cause problems for utilities that are hardcoded to reference `/etc/path_to_inst` for the device instance number file.

System utilities and diagnostic tools, like SunVTS™ software or older versions of STORtools, that must build internal tables of the devices attached to the system typically read `/etc/path_to_inst` directly, rather than obtaining the device instance information from the kernel.

Unfortunately, if these utilities hardcode the path name for `/etc/path_to_inst` into their object modules, libraries, or binaries, the path name is not easily changed. This situation prevents the use of such utilities while the client is booted from the JumpStart server or CD.

Summary

This chapter provided techniques to augment a CD-ROM-based installation with the services and behaviors provided by a JumpStart server. The techniques provided here are suitable to situations when a hands-free Solaris OE installation is necessary but when a JumpStart server cannot be used.

This chapter also detailed a procedure to create a bootable installation CD, examined the structure of a bootable Solaris OE CD, and provided specifics on the modification of the installation behaviors.

Additionally, this chapter examined the startup processing performed by the miniroot and the use of the miniroot as a platform for recovery operations. The chapter described methods and techniques to augment the startup processing to provide a framework for recovering a system. Also described were techniques for adding tools to the client's boot image.

Finally, the chapter examined the constraints of the miniroot and techniques for working within these constraints.

## CHAPTER 10

Solaris Security Toolkit

This chapter discusses the Solaris Security Toolkit (Toolkit). This Toolkit automates the process of securing Solaris Operating Environment (Solaris OE) systems. In addition to its network-based or JumpStart technology-based mode, the Toolkit can also be run in standalone mode. This chapter focuses on the parts of the Toolkit used during a network or JumpStart technology-based installation.

The Toolkit is presented here as an example of the types of problems JumpStart can solve. The development of the Solaris Security Toolkit drove the creation of several of the best practice JumpStart architecture suggestions made in this book.

This chapter describes the following Toolkit topics:

- Toolkit overview
- Toolkit architecture
- Installation and configuration of the Toolkit
- Toolkit support

Note – The Solaris Security Toolkit was formerly known as the JumpStart Architecture and Security Scripts Toolkit. It also frequently referred to by its executable name, `jass`.

Note – As in every chapter, the articles, examples, and tools mentioned, including version 0.3 of the Solaris Security Toolkit, are available on the CD-ROM included in this book.

Toolkit Overview

The Solaris Security Toolkit uses many of the JumpStart concepts described in this book to build a security toolkit that automates and simplifies the building of secured Solaris OE systems.

From a security perspective, the ideal opportunity to secure systems occurs during installation. The Toolkit works with JumpStart technology to exploit this ideal opportunity by using the JumpStart technology as a mechanism to run the security scripts in the Toolkit.

The Toolkit focuses on Solaris OE security modifications to harden and minimize a system. Hardening is the modification of Solaris OE configurations to improve the security of the system. Minimization is the removal of unnecessary Solaris OE packages from the system. These practices reduce the number of components to be patched and made secure, which in turn, can reduce entry points for potential intruders.

Note – Configuration modifications for performance enhancements and software configuration are not addressed by the Toolkit.

The Toolkit hardens systems in one of two modes: standalone or JumpStart.

Standalone Mode

The Toolkit is designed to run directly from a Solaris OE shell prompt in standalone mode. This standalone mode allows the Toolkit to be used on systems that require security modifications or updates but cannot be taken out of service for reinstallation of the OE from scratch. Ideally, systems to be secured should be reinstalled from scratch.

Standalone mode is particularly useful, however, for rehardening a system after patches have been installed. You can run the Toolkit any number of times with no ill effects on a system. Because patches can overwrite or modify files the Toolkit has also modified, always rerun the Toolkit after patches have been installed. In production environments, patches should always be staged in test and development environments before installation.

JumpStart Mode

Ideally, systems should be hardened during installation. Securing systems during the installation process integrates the implementation of your organization's security policies with the system build process. By combining these processes, you cannot overlook system hardening and so you reduce the possibility of human error and ensure consistent implementation and configuration.

Supported Versions

The current release of the Toolkit works with Solaris OE versions 2.5.1, 2.6, 7, and 8. Toolkit scripts automatically detect which version of the Solaris OE software is installed and run only tasks appropriate to that version.

Note – You should always use the most current version of the Toolkit. The most current version at the time of publication is 0.3.

Toolkit Framework

The Toolkit uses the same directory structure recommended in Chapter 2, "JumpStart Overview." When the Toolkit is installed into a directory, most of the recommended JumpStart directories are created.

The Toolkit architecture includes additional configuration information that enables scripts to be used in different environments. All variables in the Toolkit scripts are maintained in a configuration file. The configuration file is imported by a driver script that makes the variables available to all subsequent scripts.

Installing the Toolkit

When downloading the Toolkit, select the most recent version. With the release of Toolkit version 0.3, the source is being distributed in Solaris OE package stream format and as a compressed tar archive. The same source is included in both archives. How to download and install these two different archive types is discussed separately in the following sections. Future updates of this source file will be located at:

`http://www.sun.com/blueprints/tools/license.html`

Compressed Tar Archive

The instructions included below use file names that are only correct for version 0.3 of the Toolkit. Use the procedure below to download and install the Toolkit.

1. **Download the source file (**`jass-0.3.tar.Z`**) from the CD-ROM included with this book.**

2. **Extract the source file into a directory on the server by using the** `zcat` **and** `tar` **commands, as shown below:**

```
# zcat jass-0.3.tar.Z | tar -xvf -
```

Executing this command creates a subdirectory, `jass-0.3`, in the current working directory. This subdirectory contains all the Solaris Security Toolkit directories and their associated files.

Throughout the rest of this chapter the $JASS_HOME_DIR environment variable is used to refer to the root directory of the Toolkit. When the Toolkit is installed from the tar archive, $JASS_HOME_DIR is defined to be the path up to and including `jass-0.3`. If the `zcat` command described above is issued in the `/opt` directory, the $JASS_HOME_DIR environment variable is defined as `/opt/jass-0.3`.

Package Format

The instructions included in this section use file names that are only correct for the 0.3 release of the Toolkit. Use the following procedure to download and install the Toolkit.

1. **Download the source file (**`SUNWjass-0.3.pkg`**) from the CD-ROM included with this book.**

2. **Extract the source file into a directory on the server by using the** `pkgadd` **command, as shown below:**

```
# pkgadd -d SUNWjass-0.3.pkg SUNWjass
```

Executing this command creates a `SUNWjass` directory in `/opt`. This subdirectory contains all the Solaris Security Toolkit directories and their associated files. With the distributed script, `make-pkg`, administrators can create custom Toolkit packages that use a different installation directory.

The $JASS_HOME_DIR environment variable is used to define the root directory of the Toolkit. When the Toolkit is installed from the package format, $JASS_HOME_DIR is defined to be /opt/SUNWjass.

Configuration and Execution

This section details the configuration and execution of the Toolkit. You can use either of the Toolkit's two options: standalone mode or JumpStart mode.

Using Standalone Mode

In standalone mode, you can run the Toolkit directly from the $JASS_HOME_DIR directory, defined as /opt/SUNWjass in this chapter, by simply executing the following command:

```
# ./jass-execute -d secure.driver
```

Please note that this command executes all of the hardening scripts included in secure.driver. This may not be appropriate for your environment. Evaluate the security modifications your environment requires before executing the Toolkit.

By default, this script disables all remote access capabilities, such as telnet, FTP, and rlogin. Do not reboot the system, therefore, unless you have left one of those services enabled, have console access to the system, or have an alternate remote access mechanism, such as Secure Shell.

Since standalone mode requires none of the other configuration steps required for JumpStart mode, it is the quickest option to get the Toolkit up and running.

Using JumpStart Mode

For use in a JumpStart environment, copy the Toolkit source from $JASS_HOME_DIR into the base directory of the JumpStart server. Frequently, this is simply /jumpstart on the JumpStart server. Once this is done, $JASS_HOME_DIR becomes the base directory of the JumpStart server.

Typically, the Toolkit is installed in the $SI_CONFIG_DIR or base directory of the JumpStart server, for example, /jumpstart. Once installed, the $JASS_HOME_DIR environment variable is automatically set correctly.

If the Toolkit is installed under a subdirectory of $SI_CONFIG_DIR, such as $SI_CONFIG_DIR/path/to/JASS, then the following is added to the $JASS_HOME_DIR/Drivers/user.init file:

```
if [ -z "${JASS_HOME_DIR}" ]; then
        if [ "${JASS_STANDALONE}" = 0 ]; then
            JASS_HOME_DIR="${SI_CONFIG_DIR}/path/to/JASS"
        fi
fi
export JASS_HOME_DIR
```

The appropriate Toolkit driver is then added either to the rules file or to existing JumpStart finish scripts. The steps required to integrate the Toolkit into a JumpStart architecture are detailed in the remainder of this section.

1. **Copy the Toolkit source into the root directory of the JumpStart server. For example, if the Toolkit archive was extracted to** /opt/jass-0.3 **and the JumpStart server root directory is** /jumpstart, **the following command copies the Toolkit source**.

```
# pwd
/opt/jass-0.3
# cp -r * /jumpstart
```

2. **Copy the** $JASS_HOME_DIR/Drivers/user.init.SAMPLE **to** $JASS_HOME_DIR/Drivers/user.init **with the following command:**

```
# pwd
/jumpstart/Drivers
# cp user.init.SAMPLE user.init
```

3. **Now that an** user.init **file is available, change the two entries for** $JASS_PACKAGE_MOUNT **and** $JASS_PATCH_MOUNT **to the IP address of the JumpStart server.**

Note – These IP addresses are used by the JumpStart client to NFS-mount these directories during the JumpStart installation process.

Failure to modify these two IP addresses results in an error similar to the following message.

```
NOTICE: Mounting 192.168.1.5:/jumpstart/Packages on /a//tmp/jass-packages.
nfs mount: 192.168.1.5:/jumpstart/Packages: No such file or directory
NOTICE: Mounting 192.168.1.5:/jumpstart/Patches on /a//tmp/jass-patches.
nfs mount: 192.168.1.5:/jumpstart/Patches: No such file or directory
```

Remember to define the `$JASS_HOME_DIR` environment variable in the `user.init` file if the Toolkit code is not located in `$SI_CONFIG_DIR` or base directory.

Once these modifications are completed, a Toolkit driver is either selected or created and then added to the JumpStart servers `rules` file.

4. **If you are using all the scripts listed in the** `hardening.driver` **and** `config.driver`, **then add the** `secure.driver` **to the** `rules` **file. Copy the files in the** `Drivers` **directory, for example,** `secure.driver`, **and then modify them as your environment requires.**

Note – Never modify the scripts included with the Toolkit. Doing so makes migrating to a new Toolkit version much more difficult.

---

5. **One other modification may be required. If the** `sysidcfg` **files provided with the Toolkit are going to be used to automate the JumpStart client installation, review these files for correctness. If the JumpStart server encounters any errors while parsing the** `sysidcfg` **file, the entire contents of the file are ignored.**

At this point, if all the other JumpStart server specific steps have been performed it should be possible to JumpStart the client and successfully harden or minimize the Solaris OE during the installation process.

Undo Feature

The Toolkit can undo a Toolkit installation or series of installations. This feature has been added to provide administrators with an automated mechanism by which a system can be returned to its previous state.

The undo feature is only available through the `jass-execute` command in `$JASS_HOME_DIR` environment variable. Do not use the undo feature during a JumpStart installation. To undo a Toolkit run or series of Toolkit runs, use the following command.

```
# ./jass-execute -u
```

On a system where multiple Toolkit runs have been performed, output similar to the following is displayed.

```
./jass-execute: NOTICE: Executing driver, undo.driver
Please select a JASS run to restore through:
1.  May 04, 2001 at 18:25:04 (//var/opt/SUNWjass/run/20010504182504)
2.  May 04, 2001 at 18:22:50 (//var/opt/SUNWjass/run/20010504182250)
Choice?
```

The administrator can select one of these runs as the final run to undo. All system modifications performed in that selected run and any runs made after that are returned to their prior state.

Keep in mind these two important limitations of the undo feature:

1. If you selected the Toolkit option of no backup files, either through the JumpStart mode or the standalone mode, the undo feature is not available.

2. A run can only be undone once.

Once a run is undone, the backup files associated with that file are returned to their original locations. In other words, all the files backed up by a Toolkit run are restored to their original locations and are not backed up again.

The Toolkit information needed for the undo feature is logged by the Toolkit `/var/opt/SUNWjass` directory. The package name, `SUNWjass`, is the official Sun package name of the Toolkit. In this particular directory, there is a `runs` directory. For each Toolkit run, a new subdirectory in the `/var/opt/SUNWjass/runs` directory is created. It is in this subdirectory that the necessary log information for the undo feature is stored.

Note – The contents of the files in the `/var/opt/SUNWjass/runs` directory should never be modified by an administrator.

When a Toolkit run is reversed, the associated `/var/opt/SUNWjass/runs` directory is *not* removed. Instead, a new file is created in the directory indicating that the run was undone and correspondingly the undone run is not listed the next time `jass-execute -u` is executed.

Toolkit Architecture

The Toolkit architecture uses the recommended directory structure described in Chapter 2, "JumpStart Overview." This section discusses individual scripts, configuration files, or subdirectories when doing so is beneficial. The section also suggests ways to modify and add additional scripts.

Why Solaris Security Toolkit?

The default Solaris OE configuration is optimized to be a general-purpose workstation in which all services are enabled by default. The Toolkit helps secure these systems by providing an automated mechanism by which services and daemons are disabled and the optional Solaris OE security modes are enabled. By bundling this functionality with the JumpStart framework, administrators can easily incorporate security modifications into their default system builds.

For example, an unsecured Solaris 8 OE system offers approximately 30 services to the network. After configuring the Toolkit and running the `secure.driver` on this system, you have available only one service, OpenSSH. You can now customize the services that are still enabled after a Toolkit run.

Similarly, most administrators install Solaris OE systems with the `SUNWCall` cluster. On the Solaris 8 OE 4/01, this cluster contains 454 Solaris OE packages. Depending on the applications to be hosted by the system, many of these packages are not necessary. It is possible, using the scripts in the Toolkit, to build an iPlanet™ Web server with only 13 packages.

`Documentation` Directory

This directory contains all documentation discussing the security recommendations implemented by the Toolkit.

`Drivers` Directory

The files in the `Drivers` directory contain configuration information specifying what finish scripts are executed and what files are installed as a result of the Toolkit's execution. Finish scripts called by the individual driver files are located in the `$JASS_HOME_DIR/Finish` directory. Similarly, files installed by the driver files are located under the `$JASS_HOME_DIR/Files` directory.

Driver Script Creation

All driver scripts have three parts:

- The first part sets the directory path and calls the `driver.init` script. The `driver.init` script calls the `user.init` script, which contains all site-specific configuration information. The `driver.init` script then sets the environment variables that are not site specific and not defined by the `user.init` script. All subsequent Toolkit scripts use these environment variables. Note that the Toolkit will not overwrite site-specific variable assignment.

- The second part defines the `$JASS_FILES` and `$JASS_SCRIPTS` environment variables. The `$JASS_FILES` variable defines the files that are copied from the `Files` directory to the client. The `$JASS_SCRIPTS` variable defines what scripts are executed on the client. The `Finish` scripts available in the Toolkit are discussed in "Finish Scripts" on page 221.

- The third part is the `driver.run` script. This script processes the contents of the `$JASS_FILES` and `$JASS_SCRIPTS` environment variables. Based on the definition of these variables, the `driver.run` script copies files to the client and executes the selected `Finish` scripts.

FIGURE 10-1 illustrates the flow of these three parts.

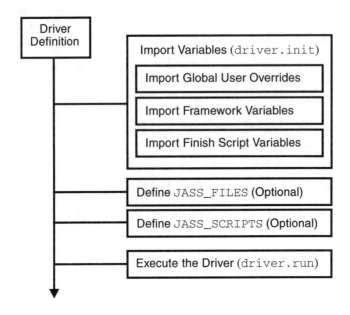

FIGURE 10-1 Driver Control Flow

All of the environment variables from the various `.init` files are imported first. Once this is complete, the driver script moves on to part two, which is the definition of `JASS_FILES` and `JASS_SCRIPTS`. The definition of these is optional; a single environment can be defined, or both, or none. Part three of the driver script calls `driver.run` to perform the tasks defined by the `JASS_FILE` and `JASS_SCRIPTS` environment variables.

The following excerpt from a driver script demonstrates the three parts.

```
DIR="'/bin/dirname $0'"

export DIR
. ${DIR}/driver.init

JASS_FILES="
            /etc/cron.d/cron.allow
            /etc/default/ftpd
            /etc/default/telnetd
"

JASS_SCRIPTS="
            install-at-allow.fin
            remove-unneeded-accounts.fin
"
. ${DIR}/driver.run
```

Driver Script Listing

The following files are in the `Drivers` directory:

- `audit.driver`
- `config.driver`
- `driver.funcs`
- `driver.init`
- `driver.run`
- `finish.init`
- `hardening.driver`
- `hardening-jumpstart.driver`
- `install-iPlanetWS.driver`
- `secure.driver`
- `undo.driver`
- `undo.funcs`
- `undo.run`
- `user.init.SAMPLE`
- `user.run.SAMPLE`

The remainder of this section discusses these critical scripts in more detail.

`audit.driver` Script

The `audit.driver` script calls all Toolkit print routines with the exception of the `print-jass-environment.fin` and `print-jumpstart-environment.fin` scripts. Use these routines to verify the configuration of a system after a Toolkit run. This script is useful when certain types of files, such as Set-UID or Set-GID binaries, need to be catalogued. By default, this script is included in the `hardening.driver` script but is commented out.

`config.driver` Script

The `config.driver` script implements a mechanism to separate scripts that perform system configuration tasks from scripts that are specific to security. Because of this separation mechanism, machines with different security requirements can still share the same base Solaris OE configuration driver.

The following is an excerpt from the `config.driver` script included with the Toolkit.

```
DIR="'/bin/dirname $0'"
export DIR

. ${DIR}/driver.init

JASS_FILES="
                /.cshrc
"

JASS_SCRIPTS="
                set-root-password.fin
                set-term-type.fin
"

. ${DIR}/driver.run
```

This script performs several tasks. First, it calls the `driver.init` script. It then sets both the `$JASS_FILES` and `$JASS_SCRIPTS` environment variables. Once the `/etc/default/sendmail` has set these environment variables, it calls the `driver.run` script. The `driver.run` script completes the installation of the specified files and executes all configuration-specific scripts.

`driver.funcs` Script

The `driver.funcs` script contains functions used by other scripts in the `Drivers` directory. To avoid the duplication of functions, separate `.funcs` files were created. This `.funcs` file contains function definitions available to other scripts.

`driver.init` Script

The `driver.init` script *must* be the first script executed by any driver script. The `driver.init` script, in combination with the `user.init` script, sets the environment variables the `Finish` scripts depend on.

`driver.run` Script

The `driver.run` script is the core of the Toolkit. All previously defined environment variables are used by the `driver.run` script to do the following:

- Verify the configuration
- Mount the filesystems to the JumpStart client (JumpStart mode only)
- Copy the files specified by the `$JASS_FILES` environment variable
- Execute scripts specified by the `$JASS_SCRIPTS` environment variable
- Unmount the filesystems from the JumpStart client (JumpStart mode only)

Each of these functions is described in more detail in this section. You can use the `user.run` script to replace or override functions or environment variables defined in the various `.run` and `.funcs` scripts.

Verifying Configuration

The `driver.run` script first verifies the Toolkit configuration by checking the following environment variables:

- `$JASS_FINISH_DIR`
- `$JASS_UNAME`
- `$JASS_STANDALONE`
- `$JASS_PATCH_MOUNT`

If these variables are not set, the verification process fails and the installation exits.

Mounting File Systems

If you are using the Toolkit in JumpStart mode, the script calls an internal subroutine called `mount_filesystems`. This routine mounts the following directories onto the JumpStart client:

- `$JASS_PACKAGE_MOUNT` — Mounts onto `$JASS_PACKAGE_DIR`
- `$JASS_PATCH_MOUNT` — Mounts onto `$JASS_PATCH_DIR`

If other filesystem mount points are required, you can use the `user.run` script to implement them.

This is a JumpStart technology-specific routine and is not executed during standalone Toolkit runs.

Copying Files

After the mounts have successfully completed, the script copies over all files specified in the `$JASS_FILES` environment variable (which can be set in any driver script) to the client. This copy mechanism is useful if you need to replace several Solaris OE configuration files during a system installation. Note that the file copy functionality is performed first so that the files are available for any finish script to use.

Executing Scripts

After the previous scripts have been executed, the finish scripts listed in the `$JASS_SCRIPTS` environment variable are executed in sequence. The output of these finish scripts is processed in one or more of the following ways:

- Logged in to the `/var/sadm/system/logs/finish.log` file on the JumpStart client during JumpStart installations. The `/var/sadm/system/logs/finish` is the standard log file used by any JumpStart command run on the client.

- Logged in to the file specified by the `jass-execute -o` option. If a file is not specified, the output is directed to standard output.

- Logged in to the file `/var/opt/SUNWjass/run/<timestamp>/jass-install.log`. The timestamp is a fully qualified time parameter in the form YYYYMMDDHHMMSS. This value is constant for each execution of the Toolkit and represents the time at which the run was started. For example, a run started at 1:30 p.m. on April 1, 2001, is represented by the value 20010401133000.

Unmounting File Systems

After running all finish scripts for the particular driver, the `driver.run` script unmounts all filesystems previously mounted (see "Mounting File Systems" on page 212) and then exits gracefully. At this point the JumpStart client reboots.

This is a JumpStart-specific routine and is not executed during standalone Toolkit runs.

`finish.init` Script

The `finish.init` script is newly added for Toolkit version 0.3. It provides a central location for the definition of finish script environment variables. Most finish scripts now offer the option to use either a hard-coded value or an environment variable defined in `finish.init` or `user.init`. Make site-specific modifications in `user.init` to simplify future migration to new Toolkit releases.

`hardening.driver` Script

The `hardening.driver` script lists all security-specific scripts included in the Toolkit. This script, similar to the `config.driver` script, defines both files and scripts to be run by the `driver.run` script.

`hardening-jumpstart.driver` Script

The `hardening-jumpstart.driver` script provides a set of scripts to successfully harden a JumpStart server. This driver is not referenced by any other driver in the Toolkit. Its only purpose is to provide a listing of the finish scripts that can be executed so that functionality required of the JumpStart server, for example, TFTP, NFS, and RPC, is still available.

`install-iPlanetWS.driver` Script

The `install-iPlanetWS.driver` script calls the `minimize-iPlanetWS.fin` script. The `minimize-iPlanetWS.fin` script removes all Solaris OE packages that are not required to successfully install and run the iPlanet web server. This updated `install-iPlanetWS.driver` script includes support for the Solaris 8 OE. Here are the contents of the driver script:

```
DIR="'/bin/dirname $0'"
export DIR

. ${DIR}/driver.init

. ${DIR}/config.driver

JASS_SCRIPTS="
minimize-iPlanetWS.fin
install-iPlanetWS.fin
"

. ${DIR}/driver.run

. ${DIR}/hardening.driver
```

If you build a JumpStart client by using this driver script, the script must be listed in the `rules` file. This `install-iPlanetWS.driver` script performs all the actions specified by the `config.driver` and `hardening.driver` scripts, in addition to the minimization functionality in the `minimize-iPlanetWS.fin` and `install-iPlanetWS.fin` scripts.

`secure.driver` Script

The `secure.driver` script is provided as a ready-to-use mechanism to implement all the hardening functionality in the Toolkit. This script performs the initialization tasks required and then calls the `config.driver` and `hardening.driver` scripts. These actions configure the system and performs all the hardening tasks specified in the `hardening.driver` script. In addition, the `audit.driver` script is listed but commented out. If the additional functionality of that script is desired, it should be uncommented. The `secure.driver` script should be the default script used in the `rules` file for the installation of clients.

The following is the content of the `secure.driver` script included with the Toolkit:

```
DIR="'/bin/dirname $0'"
export DIR

. ${DIR}/driver.init

. ${DIR}/config.driver

. ${DIR}/hardening.driver

# This is a sample driver to contain
# code for checking the status of
# various system attributes.
#
# . ${DIR}/audit.driver
```

`undo.driver` Script

The `undo.driver` implements the newly added Toolkit undo feature. This driver is straightforward and contains only the following:

```
DIR="'/bin/dirname $0'"
export DIR

. ${DIR}/driver.init

. ${DIR}/undo.run
```

When called by `./jass-execute -u`, this driver initializes itself by calling `driver.init` and then passes control to a different driver, which in the particular case above is `undo.driver`.

`undo.funcs` Script

The `undo.funcs` script and all other files in the `Drivers` directory ending with `funcs` contain functions associated with the Toolkit's undo feature but can also be used by other drivers.

undo.run Script

The undo.run script is the core of the Toolkit's undo feature functionality. It performs the following tasks:

- Imports needed functions from driver.funcs and undo.funcs
- Verifies that all of the initialization scripts have been run
- Reads any user-defined functions from user.run
- Prints identifying information about the undo run to the log file and console
- Mounts the filesystem (JumpStart mode only)
- Executes the undo_ops function to perform the undo task
- Unmounts the filesystem (JumpStart mode only)

This script is called by jass-execute when the -u option is specified.

user.init.SAMPLE Script

The user.init.SAMPLE script provides a mechanism to specify user functions that are used by the Toolkit. Use this script to override any default environment variables and to add site-specific or organization-specific information to the Toolkit, thereby minimizing future Toolkit migration issues.

This script provides default values for the $PACKAGE_MOUNT and $PATCH_MOUNT environment variables. These variables must be modified for the specific JumpStart server and directory paths required.

user.run.SAMPLE Script

The user.run.SAMPLE script is distributed as a .SAMPLE file so that it does not overwrite any user-defined scripts during an upgrade to a newer release of the Toolkit.

Use the user.run.SAMPLE script, as you would use the user.init script, to add any site-specific or organization-specific information into the Toolkit to avoid future migration issues. The user.run.SAMPLE script should contain all site-specific and organization-specific overrides for the driver.run script.

Files Directory

The Files directory in conjunction with the $JASS_FILES environment variable and the driver.run script stores the files that are copied to the JumpStart client.

The $JASS_FILES Environment Variable and Files Directory Setup

Use the $JASS_FILES environment variable to specify the complete Solaris OE path of files stored in the $JASS_HOME_DIR/Files directory. Use this environment variable in one of the following ways.

1. The first option is to specify the file that is copied from the Toolkit to the client. The following is defined in the hardening.driver script.

```
JASS_FILES="
        /etc/motd
"
```

By defining the $JASS_FILES environment variable to include this file, you replace the /etc/motd file on the client by the $JASS_HOME_DIR/Files/etc/motd file from the Toolkit's distribution. Copy any file in this manner by simply including it in the Files directory and adding it to the $JASS_FILES definition in the appropriate driver script.

2. The second option is to specify host-specific files. Do this by creating files of the following form in the Files directory:

```
/etc/syslog.conf.$HOSTNAME
```

In this example, the $JASS_HOME_DIR/Files/etc/syslog.conf file is copied only to a system with a host name that matches $HOSTNAME. When there are a syslog.conf and a syslog.conf.$HOSTNAME, the host-specific file takes precedence.

3. The third option is to specify OE release-specific files. Use this feature by creating files of the following form in the Files directory:

```
/etc/syslog.conf+$OS
```

The $OS variable should mirror the output produced by the uname -r command. If the version of the OS being secured is 5.8, then the file named $JASS_HOME_DIR/Files/etc/syslog.conf is copied. This file is not copied to any other OS release. OS-specific files have precedence over generic files but not over host-specific files.

4. The final option is to specify a directory with the `$JASS_FILES` variable. This variable copies the entire directory contents to the JumpStart client. If the `$JASS_FILES` variable contains the following line:

```
/etc/rc2.d
```

then the entire contents of the `$JASS_HOME_DIR/Files/etc/rc2.d` directory on the JumpStart server are copied to the JumpStart client.

Files Directory Listing

The following files are in the `Files` directory:

- `/etc/issue`
- `/etc/motd`
- `/etc/notrouter`
- `/etc/nsswitch.conf`
- `/etc/syslog.conf`
- `/etc/default/ftpd`
- `/etc/default/sendmail`
- `/etc/default/telnetd`
- `/etc/dt/config/Xaccess`
- `/etc/init.d/inetsvc`
- `/etc/init.d/nddconfig`
- `/etc/rc2.d/S70nddconfig`
- `/etc/security/audit_class`
- `/etc/security/audit_control`
- `/etc/security/audit_event`

The remainder of this section describes these files.

`/etc/issue` and `/etc/motd`

The `/etc/issue` and `/etc/motd` files are based on U.S. government recommendations. They provide legal notice to users that their activities may be monitored. If your organization has specific legal banners, install them into these files.

/etc/notrouter

The presence of an /etc/notrouter file disables IP forwarding between interfaces on the system. Once the JumpStart client is rebooted, the client no longer functions as a router, regardless of the number of network interfaces.

/etc/nsswitch.conf

The /etc/nsswitch.conf is an nsswitch.conf file configured so that a system uses files for name resolution. It is a copy of the /etc/nsswitch.files shipped with Solaris 8 OE.

/etc/syslog.conf

This modified /etc/syslog.conf file is installed to perform additional logging. It serves as a placeholder for organizations to add in their own centralized log server (or servers) so that proactive log analysis can be done.

/etc/default/ftpd

The /etc/default/ftpd file enables the feature available in the Solaris 7 and 8 OEs to change the default FTP banner. The banner is changed by addition of a BANNER entry to the /etc/default/ftpd file. This file, included in the Toolkit, creates a generic *Authorized Access Only* entry that denies FTP version information to potential attackers.

/etc/default/sendmail

The /etc/default/sendmail file is sendmail configuration file. With the release of Solaris 8 OE, you can use a sendmail configuration file to run sendmail in queue mode instead of cron mode. This script is copied onto the system being hardened by the disable-sendmail.fin script *only* when on a Solaris 8 OE system.

/etc/default/telnetd

The /etc/default/telnetd file enables the feature available in Solaris 7 and 8 OEs to change the default telnet banner. Change the banner by adding the BANNER entry to this file. This file, included in the Toolkit, creates a generic *Authorized Access Only* entry that denies telnet version information to potential attackers.

/etc/dt/config/Xaccess

The `/etc/dt/config/Xaccess` file disables all remote access, whether direct or broadcast, to any X server running on this system. Depending on the environment the Toolkit is used in and the X support requirements, this file may not be appropriate.

/etc/init.d/inetsvc

The `/etc/init.d/inetsvc` file replaces the default `/etc/init.d/inetsvc` with a minimized version containing only those commands required for the configuration of the network interfaces. The minimized script has only four lines as compared to the 256 lines of the Solaris 8 OE version. The minimized `inetsvc` script is as follows:

```
#!/bin/sh

/usr/sbin/ifconfig -au netmask + broadcast +
/usr/sbin/inetd -s -t &
```

Although this script is used successfully by a variety of Sun customers, it has no support for the DHCP or BIND servers. Therefore, this file should only be used in environments that use static IP assignment.

/etc/init.d/nddconfig and /etc/rc2.d/S70nddconfig

The `/etc/init.d/nddconfig` and `/etc/rc2.d/S70nddconfig` files copy over the `nddconfig` and `S70nddconfig` startup scripts required to implement specific settings.

/etc/security/audit_*

These configuration files for the Solaris OE Auditing subsystem, also referred to as the Basic Security Module, define what system and user activities are audited.

Finish Scripts

This directory contains the finish scripts that perform system modifications and updates during installation. Finish scripts are written to perform various tasks such as patch and software installation.

Finish Script Creation

During installation through JumpStart software, the finish scripts run from the miniroot loaded on the JumpStart client. The miniroot contains most of (but not all) of the Solaris OE functions.

Many of these limitations are not present during a standalone Toolkit installation, since the Toolkit is being run directly on the system being modified. This not only avoids the issues of running from the miniroot, it also removes the need for most of the chroot commands.

To simplify portability and configuration issues, the environment variables defined in the driver.init and user.init scripts are used throughout the Toolkit. If additional variables are required, they should be added as environment variables to the user.init and user.run scripts.

Finish Script Listings

Each of the scripts in the Finish directory is briefly detailed in this section. The scripts fall into the following categories:

- Disable
- Enable
- Install
- Minimize
- Print
- Remove
- Set
- Update

This list of scripts is also used in the finish script naming convention. For the latest documentation on the scripts included in the Toolkit, download the latest version of the Toolkit. See "Installing the Toolkit" on page 201 for details.

Disable Finish Scripts

Use disable finish scripts to disable services and daemons included in the Solaris OE. By default, the Toolkit disables all services enabled by default in the Solaris OE. The administrator can modify this behavior to retain (not disable) required services, such as NFS services. In addition, software should be installed to provide an encrypted administrative access mechanism, such as Secure Shell (SSH). This software ensures that the server runs only those services required instead of the many unneeded and potentially vulnerable services.

Enable Finish Scripts

Enable finish scripts modify the default configuration of the Solaris OE by enabling security features that are disabled by default. Most, if not all, new security features are disabled to ensure compliance with earlier Solaris OE releases.

Install Finish Scripts

Use install finish scripts either to install software onto the client system (for example, patches) or to create files to enable security features.

Minimize Finish Script

Minimize finish scripts remove nonessential Solaris OE packages to build systems with the absolute minimum number of the Solaris OE packages. These systems are typically dedicated to one application and have been tested for the particular hardware and the Solaris OE releases.

Print Finish Scripts

Use print finish scripts either to print diagnostic information about the environment or to search the JumpStart client for particular types of files that have a security impact.

Remove Finish Script

Use remove finish scripts to remove the Solaris OE configuration information from the JumpStart client. The modified configuration information typically removes information that either poses a security threat or is unnecessary.

Set Finish Scripts

Set finish scripts change the default values of certain variables on the client Solaris OE system.

Update Finish Scripts

Update finish scripts modify the contents of files available on Solaris OE installations. Modifications are made to these configuration files to improve the security of the system.

`Packages` Directory

The `Packages` directory contains software packages that can be installed with a finish script. For example, the *iPlanet Web Server* software package can be stored in the `Packages` directory, and from there a finish script can install the software. Usually, custom scripts need to be written to install most software packages, but the Toolkit includes a script to install the iPlanet web server.

Several finish scripts that are included in the Toolkit perform software installation and basic configuration functions. Some of these functions are described in "Finish Script Listings" on page 221.

`Profiles` Directory

The `Profiles` directory contains all profiles. The required and optional contents of profiles are discussed in Chapter 2, "JumpStart Overview." For additional information on profiles, refer to Chapter 3, "JumpStart Customizations."

Profile Configuration Files

The following profiles are included in the Toolkit:

- `32-bit-minimal.profile`
- `end-user.profile`
- `entire-distribution.profile`
- `minimal-iPlanetWS-Solaris26.profile`
- `minimal-iPlanetWS-Solaris7-32bit.profile`
- `minimal-iPlanetWS-Solaris7-64bit.profile`
- `minimal-iPlanetWS-Solaris8-32bit.profile`
- `minimal-iPlanetWS-Solaris8-64bit.profile`

Most of the profiles supplied with the Toolkit are customized for the lab environment in which the Toolkit was developed. Therefore, you can regard these profiles as samples that can be modified to suit the specific requirements of your site.

`Sysidcfg` Files Directory

This directory stores Solaris OE-specific versions of `sysidcfg` files. See "`sysidcfg` File" on page 25 of Chapter 3 for additional details. The Toolkit includes sample `sysidcfg` files for Solaris OE versions 2.5.1 through 8. These sample files are in the following directories:

- `Solaris_2.5.1`
- `Solaris_2.6`
- `Solaris_7`
- `Solaris_8`

Toolkit Support

The Toolkit was developed by Sun Microsystems engineers over a period of years. Currently, the Toolkit is available for use, subject only to the restrictions of its licensing. The Toolkit is not, at this time, a supported Sun Microsystems product. Bug support is available from the developers only as time permits. Bug reports, questions, and suggestions can be sent directly to the product developers at `jass-feedback@sun.com`.

Summary

The focus of the Solaris Security Toolkit is on the Solaris OE security modifications needed to improve the security of the Solaris OE systems through hardening and minimization. Hardening improves the security of the system, and minimization reduces the number of vulnerabilities.

Toolkit configuration allows site-specific and installation-specific modifications to the environment variables. Toolkit architecture details the directories and specific scripts. In addition, the Toolkit provides an undo capability that enables modifications to be backed out.

Solaris Security Toolkit is one of several Solaris security toolkits freely available. It is, however, the recommended Solaris OE security toolkit because it is the only one that integrates with JumpStart technology so that systems can be hardened during installation.

## CHAPTER 11

System Cloning

System cloning refers to the rapid re-creation or reinstallation of a system. It is desired that the cloned system be software-identical to the original or *master* system but not necessarily hardware-identical to the master, as long as the hardware is sufficient to perform the required tasks. When a database server is to be cloned, it is more important that the clone's software configuration be identical with the master system. It should not be a primary concern that the clone is an 8-CPU Ultra Enterprise 6500 server while the original system is a 12-CPU Ultra Enterprise 10000 server domain.

System cloning is most useful for rapid creation of replacement systems, either as a replacement for a failed or failing system or as a replacement during a disaster recovery event to ensure business continuity.

This chapter describes the following topics:

- When not to recover a system
- Overview of cloning with the JumpStart framework
- Implementation of system cloning with WebStart Flash

Using Cloning for "Disposable" Systems

With an N-Tier systems architecture, some systems fall into the category of being *commodity systems*. These commodity systems operate as stateless service providers. For an e-commerce site, the Web server front ends are an example of commodity systems.

Commodity systems can be considered disposable systems; when one of these systems fails, it is more efficient to replace the failed system. For example, having a warm standby for a Web server or using a JumpStart server to reinstall the Solaris OE and HTTP server software onto a system from a pool of spare systems can be more effective than attempting to troubleshoot or recover the failed Web server.

However, it is crucial that the commodity systems be identified and that spare systems be on hand and *burned in*. It is also crucial that you configure the JumpStart server before a failure occurs.

Additionally, to help ensure business continuity, it may be necessary to rapidly deploy systems in the event of a disaster. With an infrastructure in place to clone systems and deploy those clones, large numbers of systems can be rapidly deployed and made available to users.

Regardless of the reasons to employ system cloning, the efficient implementation of system cloning depends on the ability to identify and inventory the installed software (a software snapshot) of the master systems.

Cloning with the JumpStart Framework

To clone a system using the JumpStart framework, you need a complete software inventory and documentation of the master system disk layout. Even if the system was originally installed from a JumpStart server, its configuration and installed software may have drifted away from the installation standard over time. You can most readily obtain the current configuration information of a system by running the Sun Explorer utility on a system. Sun Explorer is available at `http://sunsolve.sun.com`. A Sun Explorer download requires a support contract and registration at SunSolve Online[SM] support.

Sun Explorer is a software utility that uses standard Solaris OE commands to query the configuration of a system and then archive the results of those queries. For example, part of the Sun Explorer output includes the results of the `pkginfo` command, providing a list of all software packages installed on the system. The Sun Explorer output also contains similar listings of installed patches and disk layout information. The output from Sun Explorer is stored in a directory hierarchy.

It is a straightforward but arduous task to develop Perl or shell scripts to parse the voluminous Sun Explorer output and generate the necessary configuration files to re-create the system from a JumpStart server. Using Sun Explorer output rather than querying a running system is recommended because the Sun Explorer output can be archived in a central location and be available if the original machine is down or unavailable. This Sun Explorer archive can be used to revert to a known functional configuration of the past.

It is outside the scope of this book to develop these scripts to extract the information necessary to generate the JumpStart `sysidcfg`, profile, and finish script to automatically re-create a system. However, by using the WebStart Flash mechanism, presented in Chapter 8, "WebStart Flash," you can easily make a software snapshot and easily clone a system. The following sections provide recommendations and detailed instructions on how to clone systems with WebStart Flash.

Implementing with WebStart Flash

The Flash archive mechanism (as described in Chapter 8, "WebStart Flash") simplifies the activity of creating and maintaining the master software snapshots. With Flash, it is only necessary to identify the already existing master machine of each system archetype that may need to be rapidly deployed and then create a Flash archive of that system. For example, you would identify and create a Flash archive of the archetype for a web server, database server, and peer-to-peer platform server, etc.

The actual implementation and deployment of the Flash archives can be done from a JumpStart server (as described in Chapter 8, "WebStart Flash") or from a disk or tape device local to the installation client.

Deploying Off-Network Systems

Deployment of clones may necessitate a mechanism to install a clone while it is off-network, either permanently or temporarily. For example, during a disaster recovery event, access to the corporate intranet and infrastructure may be severely limited *if* access is possible at all. The Flash mechanism enables the deployment of Flash archives and all the necessary files (the `sysidcfg`, `rules`, `rules.ok`, and profile) from a tape drive local to the installation client.

The following example describes how to create a Flash archive installation tape and demonstrates installing a system from that installation tape.

Creating a Flash Archive Installation Tape

For simplicity, we assume that a Flash archive has already been created as described in Chapter 8, "WebStart Flash." Create a staging area and copy or create the relevant files.

```
server01# mkdir /var/tmp/TapeStaging
server01# cd /var/tmp/TapeStaging
server01# cp /jumpstart/Sysidcfg/Solaris_8/sysidcfg .
server01# cp /jumpstart/Profiles/S8-wrkgrp-Flash.profile .
server01# cp /jumpstart/FlashArchives/S8-wrkgrp.archive .
```

The `sysidcfg` file used in this example is as follows:

```
system_locale=en_US
timezone=US/Pacific
network_interface=primary {netmask=255.255.255.0
                           protocol_ipv6=no}
terminal=vt100
security_policy=NONE
root_password=Q7anewAUage38
name_service=NONE
timeserver=localhost
```

The installation tape requires a `rules` and `rules.ok` file. Use the simplest possible `rules` file:

```
server01# echo "any - - S8-wrkgrp-Flash.profile -" >rules
server01# /jumpstart/check
Validating rules...
Validating profile S8-wrkgrp-Flash.profile...
The custom JumpStart configuration is ok.
```

Use this profile:

```
install_type     flash_install
archive_location local_tape /dev/rmt/0n 1
partitioning     explicit
#
# 4GB / and 2GB swap on a 9GB disk
#
filesys          rootdisk.s0      1201:2900          /
filesys          rootdisk.s1      1:1200             swap
```

To create a Flash archive installation tape, use `tar` and `dd` to write the configuration files and the Flash archive to the tape. Note the use of the norewind tape device in the first `tar` command. You create the tape as follows:

```
server01# mt -f /dev/rmt/0 rew
server01# tar cvf /dev/rmt/0n sysidcfg rules rules.ok \
S8-wrkgrp-Flash.profile
a sysidcfg 1 tape blocks
a rules 1 tape blocks
a rules.ok 1 tape blocks
a S8-wrkgrp-Flash.profile 1 tape blocks
server01# dd if=S8-wrkgrp.archive of=/dev/rmt/0 obs=1024000
914272+1 records in
457+1 records out
server01# mt -f /dev/rmt/0 offline
```

Note – An arbitrarily large tape block size is specified on the `dd` command. To increase performance of the tape reads during installation, use the largest possible tape block size supported by the tape drive.

To perform the installation, the clone system needs a Flash-aware miniroot. The system gets this miniroot from a Solaris 8 OE 4/01 JumpStart server or, for installing a completely off-network system, from a CD-ROM of the Solaris 8 OE 4/01 in the local CD drive.

The Flash-aware miniroot enables the boot command to recognize the tape parameter. The traditional JumpStart framework allows the `sysidcfg` file to be located only on a diskette or on a JumpStart server that is accessed through `nfs`. The Flash-aware miniroot has extensions to the JumpStart framework that enable the `sysidcfg`, `rules`, `rules.ok` and profile files to be located on a local tape.

Perform the installation from this tape as follows. The installation client is at the OBP prompt with the Solaris 8 OE 4/01 CD in the CD-ROM drive and the installation tape in the drive /dev/rmt/0.

```
{2} ok boot cdrom - install tape=/dev/rmt/0n
Initializing Memory
SunOS Release 5.8 Version Generic_108528-07 64-bit
Copyright 1983-2001 Sun Microsystems, Inc.  All rights reserved.
Configuring /dev and /devices
Using RPC Bootparams for network configuration information.
Configured interface hme0
Searching for sysid configuration file...
Using sysid configuration file from /dev/rmt/0n position 0
The system is coming up.  Please wait.
Starting remote procedure call (RPC) services: sysidns done.
Starting Solaris installation program...
Searching for JumpStart directory...
Using rules.ok from tape.
Checking rules.ok file...
Using profile: S8-wrkgrp-Flash.profile
Executing JumpStart preinstall phase...
Searching for SolStart directory...
Checking rules.ok file...
Using begin script: install_begin
Using finish script: patch_finish
Executing SolStart preinstall phase...
Executing begin script "install_begin"...
Begin script install_begin execution completed.

Processing default locales
    - Specifying default locale (en_US)

Processing profile
    - Opening Flash archive
    - Validating Flash archive


    - Selecting all disks
    - Configuring boot device
    - Using disk (c0t0d0) for "rootdisk"
    - Configuring / (c0t0d0s0)
    - Configuring swap (c0t0d0s1)
    - Deselecting unmodified disk (c0t2d0)

Verifying disk configuration
    - WARNING: Unused disk space (c0t0d0)
```
(continued on next page)

(continued from previous page)
```
Verifying space allocation
    NOTE: 1 archives did not include size information

Preparing system for Flash install

Configuring disk (c0t0d0)
    - Creating Solaris disk label (VTOC)

Creating and checking UFS filesystems
    - Creating / (c0t0d0s0)

Beginning Flash archive extraction

Extracting archive: Solaris 8 workgroup server image
    Extracted    0.00 MB (  0% of  446.42 MB archive)
    Extracted    1.21 MB (  0% of  446.42 MB archive)
    Extracted    2.19 MB (  0% of  446.42 MB archive)
                       .
                       .
                       .

    Extracted  444.06 MB ( 99% of  446.42 MB archive)
    Extracted  445.04 MB ( 99% of  446.42 MB archive)
    Extracted  446.02 MB ( 99% of  446.42 MB archive)
    Extraction complete

Customizing system files
    - Mount points table (/etc/vfstab)
    - Unselected disk mount points
(/var/sadm/system/data/vfstab.unselected)
    - Network host addresses (/etc/hosts)

Cleaning devices

Customizing system devices
    - Physical devices (/devices)
    - Logical devices (/dev)

Installing boot information
    - Installing boot blocks (c0t0d0s0)

Installation log location
    - /a/var/sadm/system/logs/install_log (before reboot)
    - /var/sadm/system/logs/install_log (after reboot)
```

(continued on next page)

```
(continued from previous page)
Flash installation complete
Executing JumpStart postinstall phase...
The begin script log 'begin.log'
is located in /var/sadm/system/logs after reboot.

syncing filesystems... done
```

Note – You can safely ignore the warning about unused disk space. The message occurs because the entire boot disk is not being used by the root filesystem. Additionally, approximately 10 Mbytes are reserved for a logical volume manager, such as Veritas Volume Manager or Solstice DiskSuite™ software.

The installation tape method is also useful in high-security datacenters or environments where systems need to be deployed with very controlled network access or completely without network access.

Summary

This chapter defined the concept of a system clone and provided an overview of using a commodity system as a replacement for recovering stateless servers. Also discussed was the use of system cloning to rapidly deploy and help ensure business continuity.

The chapter provided an overview of the use of a JumpStart server to clone systems and then described the use of WebStart Flash to clone systems, followed by details of a procedure to clone a system with Flash and without network connectivity.

Using JumpStart Technology to Install Solaris OE for Intel Architecture

This appendix presents the JumpStart server configuration files used to perform a JumpStart software installation of a client based on an Intel architecture (IA). The appendix also presents an example installation of the Solaris Operating Environment (Solaris OE) for IA.

Automated JumpStart technology of the Solaris OE for IA is recommended only for installing a large number of identical and supported x86-based systems. Individual x86-based systems can be installed with a simplified JumpStart configuration (VGA monitor and defaults for keyboard and mouse), and then a startup script can be used to run `kdmconfig`. See `http://access1.sun.com` for the x86 hardware compatibility list (HCL), and see `http://www.sun.com/intel` for additional Solaris OE for IA information.

In the following example, the JumpStart server, `server01`, is an Ultra Enterprise 420R server. The installation client, `iaclient816`, is based on an Intel Pentium II and uses a SCSI controller and a SCSI disk for the Solaris OE installation. For simplicity, this example does not use a begin or finish script or a name service. The use of these features is exactly the same as the use of the JumpStart framework to install a SPARC architecture-based system.

The Solaris 8 4/01 OE is transferred to the `/jumpstart` directory with the `setup_install_server` command:

```
server01# cd /cdrom/sol_8_401_ia/Solaris_8/Tools
server01# ./setup_install_server /jumpstart/OS/Solaris_8_2001-04_IA
Verifying target directory...
Calculating the required disk space for the Solaris_8 product
Copying the CD image to disk...
Install Server setup complete
server01# cd /tmp
server01# eject cdrom
[ insert software CD 2 of 2 ]
server01# cd /cdrom/sol_8_401_ia_2/Solaris_8/Tools
server01# ./add_to_install_server /jumpstart/OS/Solaris_8_2001-04_IA
```

The following `sysidcfg` file is used:

```
system_locale=en_US
timezone=US/Pacific
network_interface=elxl0   {netmask=255.255.255.0
                          protocol_ipv6=no}
terminal=ansi
security_policy=NONE
root_password=Q7hi0TiffztTU
name_service=NONE
timeserver=localhost
display=SUNWs3 {
        ddxHandler=ddxSUNWs3.so.1
        ddxInitFunc=SUNWs3Init
}
pointer=ps22b {
        csize=0
        buttons=2
        strmod=vuid2ps2
        ddxInitFunc=ddxSUNWmouseProc
        ddxHandler=ddxSUNWx86mouse.so.1
        dev=/dev/kdmouse
        ptrfile=ps22b.ptr
        PtrChksum=0x45cafda9
}
monitor=st3d2000pro-4 {
        device=SUNWs3
        res=1024x768
        defdepth=8
        size="20-inch (51cm)"
        board=diamond/st3d2000pro-4.xqa
        monitor=pnp/edidgen.vda
        dpix=64
        dpiy=64
        DisplayChksum=0x632aa0cf
        hz=75
        dcm=Adapter
}
```

You obtain the values for the `display`, `pointer`, and `monitor` keywords by running the command—

```
iaclient007# kdmconfig -d /var/tmp/kdmconfig.out
```

—on an Intel-based system with a similar monitor, display adapter, and mouse installed. The contents of the `kdmconfig.out` file are then appended to the `sysidcfg` file. This requires that a simplified, automated JumpStart software installation (specifying only VGA monitor and defaults for mouse and keyboard) or an interactive installation be done for the first system of each hardware configuration.

The following `rules` entry is used,

```
hostname iaclient816 \
       - \
       Profiles/S8-server-2GBroot-IA.profile \
       -
```

and the profile, `S8-server-2GBroot-IA.profile`, for this installation is

```
install_type      initial_install
system_type       standalone
fdisk             c1t0d0 solaris maxfree
partitioning      explicit
root_device       c1t0d0s0
#
# 1.5GB / and 512MB swap on a 2GB disk
#
filesys           rootdisk.s0    1474:4691       /
filesys           rootdisk.s1    1:1473          swap
cluster           SUNWCall
package           SUNWpmowm        delete
package           SUNWpmowr        delete
package           SUNWpmowu        delete
package           SUNWpmr          delete
package           SUNWpmu          delete
package           SUNWpmux         delete
```

Note the use of the `fdisk` keyword to designate the entire physical SCSI disk `c1t0d0` as a `solaris` partition, occupying the maximum amount of free space (the `maxfree` parameter). The `fdisk` keyword also implicitly designates the `solaris` partition that contains the / filesystem as the active partition (that is, the partition the system boots from). The fdisk keyword can also be used to designate only a portion of a disk to the solaris partition.

The add_install_client command used for iaclient816 is as follows:

```
server01# ./add_install_client \
> -p server01:/jumpstart/Sysidcfg/Solaris_8_IA \
> -c server01:/jumpstart iaclient816 i86pc
updating /etc/bootparams
```

Place the "Solaris 8 Device Configuration Assistant" (DCA) diskette (included with the Solaris OE for IA media kit) in the diskette drive of iaclient816, and power on the system. The installation client then boots off the DCA diskette and scans the system to determine the attached devices. By default, an Intel client prompts for permission to continue before it runs the device scan, prompts again for permission to continue before it identifies buses and devices, and then prompts for selection of the boot device. You must choose NET for a JumpStart installation. Finally, the client prompts for an interactive installation or a custom JumpStart installation; choose option 2, "custom jumpstart."

For a fully automated Solaris OE for IA installation, the profile must be placed on the DCA. Additionally, the default boot device must be specified on the DCA. This procedure for modifying the Intel boot diskette can be found in the *Solaris 8 Advanced Installation Guide*.

After the installation completes, the installation log
(`iaclient816:/var/sadm/system/logs/install_log`) from the Intel client is
as follows:

```
No capability directory found - using fallbacks.

Processing default locales
    - Specifying default locale (en_US)

Processing profile
    - Selecting cluster (SUNWCall)
    - Deselecting package (SUNWpmowm)
    - Deselecting package (SUNWpmowr)
    - Deselecting package (SUNWpmowu)
    - Deselecting package (SUNWpmr)
    - Deselecting package (SUNWpmu)
WARNING: Unknown package ignored (SUNWpmux)
    - Selecting locale (en_US)

Installing 32 Bit Solaris Packages
    - Selecting all disks
    - Configuring boot device
    - Using disk (c1t0d0) for "rootdisk"
    - Creating "maxfree" Solaris fdisk partition (c1t0d0)
    - Using existing Solaris fdisk partition (c1t0d0)
    - Configuring swap (c1t0d0s1)

Verifying disk configuration
    - WARNING: Unused disk space (c1t0d0)
    - WARNING: Change the system's BIOS default boot device for
hands-off rebooting

Verifying space allocation
    - Total software size:590.20 Mbytes

If you want to bypass the device configuration
and boot screens when the system reboots, eject
the Device Configuration Assistant/Boot diskette now.

Configuring disk (c1t0d0)
    - Creating Fdisk partition table

Fdisk partition table for disk c1t0d0 (input file for fdisk(1M))
        type: 190   active: 0    offset: 712    size: 20648
        type: 130   active: 128  offset: 21904   size: 4397480
        type: 100   active: 0    offset: 0    size: 0
(continued next page)
```

(continued from previous page)
```
      type: 100   active:  0    offset: 0    size: 0
    - Creating Solaris disk label (VTOC)

Creating and checking UFS filesystems
    - Creating / (c1t0d0s0)
/dev/rdsk/c1t0d0s0:3339992 sectors in 4691 cylinders of 4
tracks, 178 sectors
    1630.9MB in 147 cyl groups (32 c/g, 11.12MB/g, 2752 i/g)
super-block backups (for fsck -F ufs -o b=#) at:
 32, 23008, 45984, 68960, 91168, 114144, 137120, 160096, 182304,
205280, ... (list of backup superblock inodes deleted for
brevity) ...

Beginning Solaris software installation

Installation of <SUNWxwrtl> was successful.

Installation of <SUNWxwhl> was successful.

Installation of <SUNWwbapi> was successful.
              .
              .
              .
        (list of installed packages deleted for brevity)
              .
              .
              .
Customizing system files
    - Mount points table (/etc/vfstab)
          fd                   -  /dev/fd  fd    -  no -
          /proc                -  /proc    proc  -  no -
          /dev/dsk/c1t0d0s1    -  -        swap  -  no -
          /dev/dsk/c1t0d0s0  /dev/rdsk/c1t0d0s0  / ufs 1 no -
          swap                 -  /tmp     tmpfs -  yes -
    - Network host addresses (/etc/hosts)

Customizing system devices
    - Physical devices (/devices)
    - Logical devices (/dev)
Installing boot information
    - Updating boot environment configuration file
    - Installing boot blocks (c1t0d0)
```
(continued on next page)

```
(continued from previous page)
Installing unbundled device driver support

WARNING: CHANGE DEFAULT BOOT DEVICE
     If you want the system to always reboot Solaris from
     the boot device that you've specified (c1t0d0)
     without using the Configuration Assistant/Boot diskette,
     you must change the system's BIOS default boot device
     after installing Solaris software.
```

Note – To change the default boot device, use the `eeprom` command. See the `eeprom`(1M) man page for additional details.

Glossary

air gap   Two or more networks that are physically unconnected. This is a security mechanism that prevents unauthorized access in the network.

architecture   The specific design and components of a computer system and the way they interact with one another.

archive   A collection of several files bundled into one file by a program for shipment or storage.

automated installation   A feature of JumpStart that enables correctly configured JumpStart software to be automatically installed, without manual intervention, on the JumpStart client.

begin script   A Bourne shell script specified in the JumpStart server `rules` file that is executed before a Solaris Operating Environment installation begins.

boot block   An 8-Kbyte disk block that contains information used to boot a system. The boot block directly follows the disk label.

BOOTP   The boot parameter daemon and the protocol it uses.

boot server   A system that provides the services and information necessary to boot an installation client.

client/server architecture   A distributed computing architecture where one system, the server, provides information and services to another system, the client.

concatenate   To string two or more sequences, such as files, into one longer sequence.

configuration   Software options that tell computer system components how to operate.

configuration server   A system that provides the client its unique profile and software configuration. This server specifies partition sizes, the list of software to install, begin and finish scripts, etc.

cylinder	On a disk drive, the set of tracks with the same nominal distance from the axis about which the disk rotates.
daemon	A process that runs in the background, handling commands delivered for local or remote command execution.
DCA	Device Configuration Assitant.
default	A value, attribute, or option used when none has been specified.
demand-only connection	Simple security measure accomplished by removal of JumpStart entries when installation is complete.
dependent keyword	A word that specifies additional configuration details that may be required by a service or facility. Always associated with an independent keyword.
device driver	The software that converts device-independent requests into device-specific (or device-dependent) commands.
DHCP	Dynamic Host Configuration Protocol. A standard to automatically and dynamically provide an IP address to a client. One of the ways to provide a JumpStart client with its IP address.
disaster recovery	The planning and provision of datacenter services under any circumstances, even during a natural disaster such as flood or earthquake. Also referred to as Business Continuity Planning.
DNS	Domain Name System. An Internet standard service for the association and lookup of host names and IP addresses.
driver script	A script used to control the execution of multiple begin or finish scripts.
encapsulation	The method by which the Veritas Volume Manager (VxVM) software takes over management of a disk which has data that must be preserved.
finish script	A script executed after the Solaris Operating Environment installation completes.
fireridge	Another name for a firewall.
granularity	The level of detail at which something is being considered or examined.
HSFS partition	High Sierra File System partition, the standard filesystem structure used for cross-platform access to data on CD-ROMs.
HTTP	Hypertext Transport Protocol. The Internet standard that fetches hypertext objects from remote hosts.
independent keyword	A word that fully designates a service or facility and does not require a dependent keyword to provide additional configuration specifications.
install server	The source of software packages that are to be installed on the client.

installation client	The system on which the Solaris Operating Environment is to be installed. The installation client can be any hardware platform capable of running the Solaris Operating Environment, including those hardware platforms typically referred to as servers.
interactive installation	An installation of the Solaris Operating Environment done manually, with interaction from the person installing the system.
IA platform	Intel-architecture platform.
IP address	A unique 32-bit number that identifies each host on a TCP/IP network.
Kerberos	A network authentication protocol developed by the Massachusetts Institute of Technology.
kernel	The core of the operating system software. The kernel is the lowest software level and runs directly on the hardware. The kernel manages all system resources and implements fundamental software services, such as virtual memory management, that the hardware may not provide.
kernel architecture	The classification of a kernel based upon the kernel's hardware-specific portion, for example, sun4u for the Sun Fire systems.
keyword	A specific or predefined word or phrase in a document or record that is used in accessing, sorting, or searching.
LDAP	Lightweight Directory Access Protocol. A name service.
MAC	Media Access Control. An Ethernet address.
man pages	UNIX online documentation.
master machine	The system that serves as the template to be copied onto the installation clients.
miniroot	A Solaris Operating Environment kernel that provides minimal kernel services. The miniroot is independent of the the hardware architecture.
name services	In a general sense, a repository that organizes and names objects. It provides an association, often referred to as a binding, between a name and an object.
network segmentation	A security mechanism that uses a physically separated network to isolate network traffic.
NFS	Network File System. Sun's distributed computing filesystem.
NIS	Network Information Service. Sun Microsystems' distributed name service.
NIS+	Network Information Service Plus. A hierarchical name repository that is a successor to NIS.

N-Tier architectures	A datacenter architecture where well-defined system types are provided in tiers. N-Tier architectures permit segmentation of servers.
OBP	OpenBoot PROM (programmable read-only memory). The system firmware.
OpenBoot PROM	See OBP.
OS	Operating system. A collection of programs that control the use of the hardware and supervise the other programs executed by the system.
patches	Updates and enhancements to the Solaris Operating Environment or application software.
physical cable connection	A security mechanism that promotes a secure network environment by omitting a physical cable connection between a JumpStart environment and a client.
RARP	Reverse Address Resolution Protocol.
RAS	Reliability, Availability, and Serviceability.
rules file	A text-based configuration file that contains a rule for each group of systems (or a single system), and that also contains information on configuring and installing the Solaris Operating Environment.
second-level network boot process	The software loaded by the OBP after the system firmware completes its Power On Self-Test (POST). The second-level boot process is responsible for booting the Solaris Operating Environment.
snapshot	A point-in-time copy of a system or disk.
Solaris Security Toolkit	This Toolkit is designed to automate the process of securing Solaris Operating Environment systems.
SSH	Secure Shell.
SSP	System Service Processor. The system responsible for the management of an Ultra Enterprise 10000 frame.
staging environment	A network environment used for the prebuiliding, burn-in, testing, and integration testing of systems and services before the systems and services are moved to their appropriate location on the network.
standalone mode	The term applied to the method of running the Solaris Security Toolkit directly from a Solaris Operating Environment shell prompt.
sysidcfg file	A configuration file that provides the necessary client information for an automated JumpStart installation.
TFTP	Trivial File Transfer Protocol.

validate To have an application verify that the contents of a text field are appropriate to the function.

VTOC Volume Table of Contents. The location on a disk drive where the disk geometry and partitioning information is stored.

VxVM VERITAS Volume Manager.

WAN Wide Area Network. A network consisting of many distributed systems. This network can cover a large physical area, sometimes worldwide.

Index

Boot Server:

- bootp or DHCP
- (install => boot net - install)

Configuration Server:

SOLARIS™ SECURITY TOOLKIT
LICENSE AGREEMENT

BY OPENING THIS SEALED SOFTWARE MEDIA PACKAGE,
YOU ACCEPT THE LICENSE AGREEMENT BELOW:

The Solaris[tm] Security Toolkit is a tool designed to assist in creation and deployment of secured Solaris[tm] Operating Environment systems. The Toolkit is comprised of a set of scripts and directories implementing the recommendations made in the Sun BluePrints OnLine program (http://www.sun.com/blueprints).

These scripts can be executed on Solaris Operating Environment systems through the JumpStart™ technology or directly from the command line. The Toolkit includes scripts to harden, patch, and minimize Solaris Operating Environment systems.

Sun does *not* support the Toolkit.

DISTRIBUTION: Only Sun Microsystems, Inc. ("Sun") or an authorized Sun VAR may distribute the Toolkit in any form. Once a party other than Sun or an authorized Sun VAR is in possession of the Toolkit, it may not further distribute the Toolkit, either directly or indirectly, in any form, modified, original, or otherwise, to any third party.

LICENSE GRANT: Sun hereby grants a non-exclusive, non-transferable and royalty free license to use, reproduce, and modify the Toolkit for the following internal purposes only (no license is granted for any other purpose):

1. Your internal research use;

2. Your internal evaluation of the Toolkit;

3. Your internal use only, for the purposes of running your business or otherwise.

Other than the licenses expressly granted in this license grant, Sun retains all right, title, and interest in the Toolkit.

DISCLAIMER OF WARRANTIES: THIS TOOLKIT IS OFFERED "AS IS" AND "WITH ALL FAULTS" AND WITHOUT WARRANTY OF ANY KIND WHATSOEVER. SUN DISCLAIMS, AND USERS OF THE TOOLKIT WAIVE, ANY AND ALL EXPRESS OR IMPLIED WARRANTIES AND REPRESENTATIONS, INCLUDING BUT NOT LIMITED TO ANY IMPLIED WARRANTY OF MERCHANTABILITY, FITNESS FOR A PARTICULAR PURPOSE, OR NON-INFRINGEMENT. THE TOOLKIT IS TO BE USED AT YOUR OWN RISK.

NO LIABILITY: IN NO EVENT SHALL SUN BE LIABLE FOR ANY DIRECT, INDIRECT, PUNITIVE, SPECIAL, INCIDENTAL, OR CONSEQUENTIAL DAMAGE IN CONNECTION WITH OR ARISING OUT OF THE USE OF THE TOOLKIT (INCLUDING, BUT NOT LIMITED TO, LOSS OF BUSINESS, REVENUE, PROFITS, USE, DATA, OR OTHER ECONOMIC ADVANTAGE) HOWEVER IT ARISES, WHETHER FOR BREACH OR IN TORT, EVEN IF SUN HAS BEEN PREVIOUSLY ADVISED OF THE POSSIBILITY OF SUCH DAMAGE.